In 1974, sitting in his office in a truck company in Sydney, John Marsden noticed a small newspaper advertisement for a teaching course. Bored and frustrated by his job, John applied for the course, was accepted, and began teaching in 1978. In his first year he taught P.E., Remedial Reading, and curated the First XI cricket pitch. Just as the year started he was also given an English class of feral Year 10s, who put him through a gruelling survival course in classroom management.

John survived, and by 1984 he was Head of English at Geelong Grammar's famous Timbertop campus.

Three years later John's first novel was published. *So Much to Tell You* became one of Australia's most successful books, selling half a million copies and being translated into twelve other languages. A string of international hits followed, including *Letters from the Inside, Tomorrow, When the War Began, Checkers*, and *Dear Miffy*.

But John has always remained committed to teaching, and he now runs writing workshops on a property near Romsey, in Victoria. This new edition of *Everything I Know About Writing*, with its lively fresh style and brilliant new insights, is evidence of how successfully John combines his twin careers of writing and teaching.

You can visit John Marsden's website at:

www.johnmarsden.com.au

T0358004

## Also by John Marsden

So Much to Tell You
The Journey
The Great Gatenby
Staying Alive in Year 5
Out of Time
Letters from the Inside
Take My Word for It
Looking For Trouble
Tomorrow . . . (Ed.)
Cool School
Creep Street
Checkers
For Weddings and a Funeral (Ed.)
This I Believe (Ed.)
Dear Miffy
Prayer for the 21st Century
Everything I Know About Writing
Secret Men's Business
The *Tomorrow* Series 1999 Diary
The Rabbits
Norton's Hut
Marsden on Marsden
Winter
The Head Book
The Boy You Brought Home
The Magic Rainforest
Millie
A Roomful of Magic
The Year My Life Broke
South of Darkness
The Art of Growing Up

The *Tomorrow* Series
Tomorrow, When the War Began
The Dead of Night
The Third Day, the Frost
Darkness, Be My Friend
Burning for Revenge
The Night is for Hunting
The Other Side of Dawn

*The Ellie Chronicles*
While I Live
Incurable
Circle of Flight

# EVERYTHING I KNOW ABOUT WRITING

# John Marsden

**PAN**

Pan Macmillan Australia

First published 1993 by Reed Books.
This edition first published 1998 in Pan by Pan Macmillan Australia Pty Limited
1 Market Street, Sydney

Reprinted 1999, 2000, 2003, 2004, 2006, 2009, 2010 (twice)

Copyright © John Marsden 1993

The moral right of the author has been asserted.

National Library of Australia
Cataloguing-in-Publication data:

Marsden, John, 1950– .
Everything I know about writing.

ISBN 978 0 330 36073 9

1. English language–Rhetoric.  2. Creative writing I. Title.

808.042

Typeset in 11/13 pt Baskerville by Midland Typesetters Pty Ltd
Printed by IVE

# ACKNOWLEDGEMENTS

Wherever possible I've credited people whom I've quoted, or from whom I've picked up topics or ideas. Sometimes though my filing system hasn't yielded names or sources. I apologise to those who've been overlooked in that way.

I do know, however, that I want to thank Elizabeth and Andrew Farran for dogged and skilful typing; and Tash Hecher, Hamish Cameron, Tom Watson, Anna Brown, Michael Long, Rhys James, Jill Montague, J. Wilson Hogg, Julia Stiles, Michelle John, Charlie Bell, Jeff Phillips, Matt Hamilton, Tori Woodhouse, Pradeep Wijayapala, Sam Marsden, Natalie Deans, Poss Herbert, Kirsty Mitchell, Raynor Tom, Andrew Mayne, John Lewis, Agnes Nieuwen-huizen, and Peter McCarthy, for various contributions not always specifically acknowledged in the text.

In particular I'd like to thank two friends and ex-colleagues, Dr John Goddard and Dick Johnstone, whose collections of language gaffes supplied me with a number of examples used in this book.

Finally I wish to thank the Literature Board of the Australia Council, for generous financial assistance.

## DEDICATION

*In my primary, secondary and tertiary schooling I had some terrible teachers, a lot of mediocre ones, and a few who were wonderful. Among this last group were: Mrs Marjorie Scott, Mr Tom Baddiley, Mr Robert Parker and Mr Nigel Krauth.*

*This book is dedicated to them, with thanks for their encouragement, support and inspiration.*

# CONTENTS

PART THREE:

# 600 Writing Topics

# PART ONE

# The Collector

# Introduction

Some people collect thimbles, some collect old cars, some, believe it or not, collect telephone cards, but the person who wants to be a better writer has to be a collector of language.

The English writer A.S. Byatt put it like this: 'You can't speak your own language properly if you don't have a storehouse of singing things in your mind.'

All good writers and readers, consciously or unconsciously, are aware of language. They respond strongly when they see or hear language used beautifully, cleverly and effectively. These are the 'singing things' referred to by A.S. Byatt.

And they respond strongly to language used in an ugly or clumsy or confusing way – a badly chosen word, an awkward image – just as a gardener winces at the sight of weeds choking an orchid, or a farmer is distressed to see footrot in a mob of sheep.

You must develop this sensitivity, too, and become a student of language! Then you will start to realise what works and what doesn't, what's fresh and what's stale, what's beautiful and what's not.

The process works like this: first you take an interest in language, after a while you become sensitive to it, finally you become expert in it. The aim is to use words with facility and skill. Just as the good gardener can spot a weed at a hundred metres on a dark night, and the good farmer can tell at a glance which sheep in the mob are not walking easily, so the language expert can immediately identify the failing sentence or the unsatisfactory word, and correct or improve it.

Being a language-collector is a fun hobby! Yes, even more fun than collecting telephone cards, if you can believe that. I'm constantly writing down examples of good and bad language in my notebooks. This means eavesdropping at bus stops and in supermarkets, reading billboards and street signs, listening attentively and critically to radio and television.

I'm not sure how this interest developed. I remember enjoying the sound of the words in some of the poems I read as a child:

**Jonathan Jo**
**Has a mouth like an 'O'**
**And a wheelbarrow full of surprises;**
**If you ask for a bat,**
**Or for something like that,**
**He has got it, whatever the size is.**

That was one favourite. This was another:

**They're changing guard at Buckingham Palace**
**Christopher Robin went down with Alice.**
**Alice is marrying one of the Guards.**
**'A soldier's life is terrible hard,'**
**Says Alice.**

They're both by A. A. Milne, from *When We Were Very Young*.

My father used to amuse us with snippets of funny language:

**Q: What's the difference between a duck?**
**A: One of its feet is both the same.**

and:

**A queer bird is the pelican,**
**Its beak holds more than its stomach is able to.**

One of the reasons we found this funny was that it avoided saying 'belly', which in those days was considered a rude word.

I loved rhythms and rhymes. By the age of nine I was haunted by the poignancy of Irene McLeod's 'Lone Dog':

**I'm a lean dog, a keen dog, a wild dog and lone;**
**I'm a rough dog, a tough dog, hunting on my own;**
**I'm a bad dog, a mad dog, teasing silly sheep;**
**I love to sit and bay the moon, to keep fat souls from**
**sleep.**

On long boring car trips I amused myself by reading the clever language of billboards, so often based on puns, onomatopoeia or alliteration:

**Better late than dead on time.**

**Next to myself I like BVDs best.**

**... Sssssschweppervesence ...**

**Better buy Buttercup Bread.**

These days, if you walk into my house you won't have to look far to realise my interest in language. On a bookshelf conveniently placed within arm's length of the desk are thirty or forty dictionaries, most in constant use. They include dictionaries of quotations, proverbs, idioms, foreign languages, phrases and fables, synonyms, abbreviations and Australian English; and etymological dictionaries. I have seven dictionaries of slang and colloquialisms. By taking such an interest in language I'm sure that I've improved my English; it helps me lift my standards and avoid making the mistakes that, although easy to make, are so damaging to one's writing.

The English language is my number one hobby!

It is a useful exercise to write a personal history of your involvement with the English language as I've done briefly here. Go back to your earliest memories of words and phrases, and consider the effect of different pieces of language on you. Continue your essay right through to today, quoting recent examples of language that has made an impact on you.

# Good English

To some extent what we call 'good' is a personal response. But often there's general agreement, when most people who encounter a particular group of words are impressed by them.

Certainly though, not everyone would agree that the informal language used by school students is 'good English'. I think it often is. It can be fresh, colourful, poetic. It's changing all the time too, and if you don't keep up to date you can feel that you're not a member of the group.

This shows us one important function of language: that it can determine who's in a community and who isn't. For example, most private school students call their canteen a tuckshop. Most government school students call it a canteen. If you were to change from one system to the other, you'd have to learn the language of the new school. Until you did, you'd be branded an outsider.

Hundreds of the examples of language I've collected over the years come from schools. Here's one from a bus-load of Year 12 boys I was driving to a tennis match. The conversation went like this:

Jeff: 'Are you still with Sarah?'
Matt: 'Oh no, mate, I crashed and burned so badly Saturday night.'

Crashed and burned! A perfect description of what happens when you wreck a relationship! A few weeks later, the expression had been abbreviated to 'c. and b.':

'How's Teresa?'
'C. and b. mate, c. and b.'

Poetic and succinct. There was a craze a while ago for giving names to people who were thought to be unpopular: names like Scott (for 'S'cott no friends'), Wes ('Wes all your friends?'), Neville ('S'cott no friends and Neville will') and Nigel. I never worked out where Nigel came from.

Other students' words I liked were 'strap' for cheating ('She strapped my essay'), 'lag' for dobbing ('He's such a lagger!' 'Did you lag on me?'), and 'pussburgers' for those meat-and-cheese-covered-in-breadcrumbs concoctions they sell in supermarkets.

A favourite word in a boarding school where I taught was 'maggot'. A social maggot was someone who gossiped all day and never did much else. So conversations like this were quite common:

**'Have you seen Tom?'**
**'Oh, he's such a social maggot, he's probably on the library lawn again.'**

After a while the students started using it as a verb; for example, 'I think I'll go maggoting for a while.' As I was going into the staff room for morning tea a student called out, 'Happy maggoting, sir!' I heard one girl say, rather poignantly: 'My parents sent me to boarding school so they could go maggoting in Melbourne.'

Some of my favourites have been 'one-offs'. A girl complaining about her teacher said with a sigh: 'She's such a stress monster.' One time I walked past two girls, one of whom was hesitating about approaching a boy she liked. Her friend was encouraging her: 'Go for gold, Tori! Go for gold!' I used that line in a book. I remember a boy called Pradeep, looking at the wreck of a model plane that had crashed, and saying, with a sympathetic click of the tongue, 'Oh! Crumpulations, dudes.' And a Year 9 girl trying to get some boys to move, finally complained to me: 'They're being such boy-y people.' On each of these occasions I've rushed for my notebook.

A lot of the expressions used by school students are unmentionable here, unfortunately, and a lot of these are insults. Would it be true to say that ninety per cent of insults hurled in schools are the same five or six words? That makes for pretty boring language. I like the way 'The Young Ones' on television were given such novel insults to use: 'bottom boil' is one I remember, 'farty-breath' was another. Fresh insults are much more potent (they often defuse the tension, too). Books like *All right, Vegemite* have shown just how rich the 'rude' language and insults of school students can be.

This is a conversation I heard in a school:

'My brother's a pain.'
'My brother goes beyond pain.'

Here's another one, from Devonport, Tasmania:

'Haven't you got a brain?'
'No, when God handed them out I thought they were milk shakes, and I asked for an extra thick one.'

And one more:

'You're making me sick.'
'Fine then, go and be sick.'

Sometimes specialist magazines for young people deliberately exaggerate the unique language of teenagers to get an effect. Here's a letter from the *Dolly* Pen-Pals page:

'Chow down spacos! Drop your macka lot at our wooden box if you wanna cool it and show what a ripping spagnoli your troppo self is. We are two funky doodettes who crack up at the zapagorny attitude of quaverial life. So write marbot! ACT.

That was one occasion when all my forty dictionaries failed me.

# Good English in Poetry

It can be argued that poets use language better than anybody. Certainly I read a lot of poetry, savouring the elegance and economy of its language, moved by the beauty with which poets choose and arrange words. The discipline which poetry demands helps produce many perfect statements, that have enriched our culture.

**He nothing common did or mean**
**Upon that memorable scene.**

This is seventeenth-century poet, Andrew Marvell, describing the behaviour of the English King Charles I as he walked to his execution. Discipline is evident, not just in the choice of words compressing the image into two lines, but also in the emotional restraint shown by the writer. It's dignified, touching and noble.

In his play, *Antony and Cleopatra*, William Shakespeare describes Cleopatra's barge:

**The barge she sat in, like a burnished throne,**
**Burned on the water: the poop was beaten gold;**
**Purple the sails, and so perfumed that**
**The winds were love-sick with them; the oars were silver,**
**Which to the tune of flutes kept stroke, and made**
**The water which they beat to follow faster,**
**As amorous of their strokes.**

The way in which the poet uses the word 'burned' in the second line to reflect 'burnished' is a delight, as is the image of the wind in love with the perfumed sails, and the image of the water in love with the strokes of the oars.

Sometimes a poet will take a profound truth and express it with marvellous simplicity; as in Thomas Gray's 'Elegy written in a Country Churchyard':

The boast of heraldry, the pomp of pow'r,
And all that beauty, all that wealth e'er gave;
Awaits alike th' inevitable hour.
The paths of glory lead but to the grave.

The power of the last line, after the slightly florid language of the first three, hits like an express train. These plain, sobering words could be painted above the entrance to every Parliament House in this country.

In recent years reading poetry has been less popular; listening to songs has replaced it for many people. But it's almost the same thing: a lot of songs are poems set to music. Songwriters like Bob Dylan, Lennon and McCartney, Paul Simon, Tracy Chapman, Don Walker (Cold Chisel), Paul Kelly, Judy Small and Eric Bogle are among our best poet/musicians. The Bruce Springsteen song 'Born in the USA' reflects a society where many people are beaten before they start:

Born down in a dead man's town
The first kick I took was when I hit the ground
You end up like a dog that's been beat too much
Till you spend half your life just covering up ...

and later:

Down in the shadow of the penitentiary
Out by the gas fires of the refinery
I'm ten years burning down the road
Nowhere to run, ain't got nowhere to go ...

The lines punch hard, with a fresh strong image in each one, and in between them the ironic chorus, 'I was born in the USA', a phrase more commonly touted as a mark of pride than the badge of oppression and defeat that Springsteen suggests.

# Good English in Sport

Although sports commentators are among the worst users of English in our society, frequently throttling the language until it's black in the face, people involved in sport sometimes do show a special feeling for words. Maybe it happens when they apply the skills needed in sport to their speaking and writing. After all, the people who do best in sport are those who combine directness with subtlety, who show discipline, yet still have individual style and imagination ... and what better principles than those for communicating!

Here's Terry Wheeler, ex-coach of the AFL Western Bulldogs team:

**There are no trees on a football field, no rocks, nowhere to hide.**

I find that stark, direct and powerful.

When Australian cricketer David Boon was hit on the chest by a rising ball, Max Walker gave this vivid prediction of Boon's bruises:

**He'll have a receipt for a couple of days, no doubt about that. The rings of Saturn will come out – green, purple, a sort of murky grey ...**

And this is swimmer Tracey Wickham, talking about her disciplined approach:

**There was one girl I used to swim against. She'd stand up there on the blocks beside me and I'd be one hundred per cent serious and blocking everything out and here she'd be, this pretty blonde thing, winking at the boys and yapping away to me, saying things like, 'Gee, Tracey, I like your hair.' I like your hair! I'd think, No wonder you never do any good, your mind's all over the place. You're in the wrong place, kid. Go and do ballet or something.**

I'm not suggesting that Tracey's going to pick up any writing awards but there's something special about her language. And it's this: her voice comes through so powerfully. We know that we are hearing her self. It is authentic. As well, it's lively and engaging: a strong expression of her attitudes.

Skateboarding and surfing, in particular, are full of wonderful expressions. Why is this, I wonder? Words like grommet, skeg and bail (surfing), and ollie, acid drop, faceplant (ouch!), tick-tock, slam and stalefish (skateboarding) – these sports have a strong, fluid, fascinating language of their own. Is there some special reason for this? (Cricket, for example, has a very complex language, but it hardly ever changes.)

If sport is a strong interest in your life, then extend your interest to include the language of sport. It has its own style.

# Good English and Little Kids

Children who are three or four years old often use English in an original and colourful way. Unfortunately they get laughed at so often that they soon conform to the same boring and predictable patterns as the rest of us. But a lot of my favourite pieces in my language collection come from very young children.

A friend of mine, Kirsty, was baby-sitting a five-year-old. The little girl had an infant brother who'd been born blind. One day Kirsty was taking the five-year-old for a walk through the paddocks, when the child said to her:

**'Kirsty, that black cow, and the sky at night, and my baby brother are all alike.'**

That's a moving and poetic description of blindness.

A teacher was telling me about his son, who at the age of four was in love with a little girl at his kindergarten. He announced it to his father by saying:

**'Daddy, I'm enheartened with Sophie.'**

Enheartened! You won't find that meaning in any dictionary but it's a beautiful use of the word.

I was once told about a child who changed 'got' from a verb to a noun. Whenever he found anything especially good, that he wanted to show people, he'd go around with it in his hand, saying proudly, 'Look at my got, look at my got!'

If you have a little brother or sister, try eavesdropping on them for a while.

# Good English and Comedians

What percentage of jokes in our society are based on language? Forty per cent? Fifty per cent? In fact, if you added language jokes to jokes about fearful and taboo subjects (sex, excretion, pain, death) you'd just about have covered them all.

Comedians are nearly always brilliant users of language. There are simple but clever jokes like these:

**Q: What do you call an Eskimo's home if it doesn't have a toilet?**
**A: An ig.**
**Q: What do you call a fly with no wings?**
**A: A walk.**
**Q: What do you get from baked beans and onions?**
**A: Tear gas.**

Then there is the sophisticated humour of people like Andrew Denton and Rita Rudner, comedians who manipulate words to trick and delight us, or of Red Symons asking poignantly on 'Hey Hey It's Saturday': 'How come when I go out, a lot of people wave to me, but they don't use all their fingers?' That's a beautifully constructed sentence, with the sting in its tail. Other examples I can think of include a Ronnie Barker/Ronnie Corbett sketch about a party where there's only one guest, who gets a choice of water or melted ice to drink and offers to play sardine as a party game, after commenting that he 'can't stand sitting down'; a postcard with the statement, 'If only I could relate to people I'm related to!'; and this, from 'The Goon Show', where some would-be archaeologists are excavating a site:

Crun: 'What are you doing Min? The dog's had four bones already, three of them mine ... Ahh, look, another one ... Ahh, look!'

Minnie: 'Oh, Lord Crun ... This skull is five million years old.'

Henry (sings): 'Happy birthday to you, Happy birthday to you ... '

All of these are language jokes, as is this entry to a newspaper competition for opening paragraphs of detective stories:

Four a.m. Friday morning. I was in my office working on a case. I had to work on a case, I couldn't afford a desk. There was a tap at the door. I got up and turned it off. I hate to see waste. On the way back I saw a figure pass my window. This was one tall broad – my office is on the second floor. She arrived at my office door, a live brunette. This dame spelt trouble. She got it right first time. I asked her to spell psychiatrist. Not now, she said. She fell into my office and leaned close to me over my case. I could see it was murder, she had it written all over her face. I passed her a Kleenex so she could wipe it off and she warned me about the hood in the alley-way with the felt-tip. Then she broke down and spilled her guts. I could see this one was going to need a lot of Kleenex.

Few people have had the understanding and skill in language that Spike Milligan possesses. Having mastered English when young, he has been making it do anything he wanted ever since, constantly remoulding it and sending it into fresh territories. Here's a sample from his book, *Adolf Hitler: My part in his downfall.* He's describing the snorers in his Army barracks during World War II:

**Each one had his own unique sound. Gunner Forest's was like gargling with raw eggs through a gently revolving football rattle. For sheer noise, Gunner Notts. He vibrated knives, forks and spoons on the other side of the room. Before he went to sleep we secured all the loose objects with weights. Syd Price gave off snores so vibrant, his bed travelled up to six inches a night. On bad nights we'd find it out in the passage. Next, the teeth grinders! Gunner Leech's was like a dry cork twisting in the neck of a bottle, followed by the word,'fissss-sashhhhhhhh' ...**

People who just recite jokes all day – 'There was this kangaroo hopping down a road ... ' 'Knock, knock ... ' 'Why did the fireman take a fishing line to the ... ' – can get quite boring. Often the really funny people are the ones who are quick with language and have an ability to use words in clever and fresh ways. I remember a Year 7 boy named Raynor. He walked into a room one day where some kids were fooling around with a condom. 'What's that?' Raynor innocently asked. There were immediate howls of derision, but Raynor, realising his mistake, recovered beautifully: 'I know what it is,' he said. 'I've just never seen one that small before.'

## Good English in all Kinds of Places

In a woodwork room in a secondary school a teacher had posted a set of rules on the board. The first two rules were these:

IF YOU MOVED IT, YOU PUT IT BACK.
IF YOU DIDN'T MAKE IT, DON'T TOUCH IT.

To me this is perfect English. There's no clutter of words, no jargon, no confusion of meaning. This is language at its most powerful.

There's no telling where new specimens of good language will appear. They can even come from mis-spellings. A boy called Andrew in my Year 10 class handed in an essay about Surfers' Paradise, which he'd spelt as Surface Paradise. I thought his spelling error was a brilliant description of the place. Another student, describing a violent storm, accidentally crossed the 'l' in 'lightning' and made it a 'tightning storm'. That was a much better word. It gave an image of a storm tightening its grip on a district: ominous black clouds, growling thunder, suffocating stillness.

When a boy who'd recently left our school was killed in a car crash, a crash which his passenger survived, the Principal broke the news to us, and one of his sentences was so beautiful that I wrote it down. He said, 'Peter handled the car in such a way that Andrew was preserved, but he himself was not.' The gravity and grace with which this sentence was delivered made a deep impression on me.

A friend of mine went in to a fruit shop. She saw some small black berries there, but she couldn't identify them. So she asked the fruiterer: 'What are those?' He replied: 'They're blueberries, but they're black because they're green.'

It makes sense, when you think about it.

Yes, good language is all around us. By becoming more aware of it, we improve our own skills. We start to fill the mind with singing things.

# Bad English

Let's face it, finding fault with others is fun – why else would so many people become teachers?

But there's nothing quite so efficacious as identifying your own and other people's mistakes. You become conscious – very quickly – of all the common faults, and from there it's but a small step to eliminating them from your own speech and writing.

You have to train yourself to be a critical reader and a critical writer. Take this headline, for instance, from the Melbourne *Age* newspaper: 'Israelis Shoot Dead Arab Boy'. Ask yourself, 'Is that the best way of conveying the main point of the story? Could it have been better worded? Isn't it ambiguous?'

# Tautologies

Getting rid of clutter is important, if not in a first draft then when you edit. A lot of clutter consists of tautologies – words that unnecessarily repeat what you've said. Here's an example from a television programme called 'Lateline' in which a financial expert was discussing the Foster's company.

**It's the fourth biggest brewer in the world and there's only three brewers ahead of it.**

Here's another, from a newspaper article, where a Mr Carruthers was talking about Parramatta Jail. He said he thought it was a very relaxed type of jail, then added this sentence:

**However, there are always hidden factors which one cannot see out in the open.**

On 3MP radio news one day came this statement:

**The foreign minister, Senator Evans, left Australia today for overseas.**

3MP must have a tautology specialist on the staff, as they were responsible for this one too:

**Mr Packer's heart stopped, and he lost consciousness.**

I thought the second half of the sentence was a bit unnecessary.

Cricket commentators are legendary tautologists.

**This is one of the great cricket grounds in the world, to play cricket on. (Tony Greig)**

**Well, the day began this morning ... (Tony Greig again)**

**He's about six foot three in height. (Bob Willis)**

**He's been having nightmares at night about that. (Max Walker)**

**The clouds are still about, in the sky. (South African commentator)**

But even institutions famous for their 'correct' English can slip.

**... and a dawn raid by police and social workers, early in the morning. (BBC Radio 4)**

**Lamont derided as a Chancellor who dreams dreams. (Headline in the *Times*, June 14, 1991)**

What else can you dream, if not dreams?

# Ambiguity

Sometimes a sentence is so poorly written that it can be read two possible ways and the reader is left confused.

**'Her eyes flew open, and she saw his fly open too.' (Mills and Boon novel)**

I had a very literate dog named Alby. One day he sneaked into the Staff Room at the school where I worked. The cleaners had left a big sign saying 'WET FLOOR'. So he did.

At the Seoul Olympics the diving commentators informed us:

**'Some of these divers are having trouble getting into the pool.'**

Trouble getting into the pool! That's serious for a diver! The commentators meant that the divers were splashing too much as they entered the water, and thus losing points.

# Mixed Metaphors

**Zivojinovic seems to be able to pull the big bullet out of the top drawer. (Tennis commentator)**

What was the big bullet doing in the top drawer? The commentator got confused when using the language of metaphor (indirect comparison). He could have said, 'He's able to play shots from the top drawer', or 'He's able to fire the big bullet'. Both are well-known (in fact, rather stale) expressions. But in the heat of the moment he mixed them and made a mess.

A CD review in the *Age* newspaper included this sentence:

**'The Moon and You' ... is a highpoint, Grabowsky says, perhaps even a watershed for modern Jazz, bringing it into the mainstream by the back door.**

Now I don't know much Geography but I do know it's difficult to bring a watershed into a mainstream by a back door.

In January 1998, when Shane Warne took his 300th Test wicket, captain Mark Taylor reminisced:

**Back in South Africa Shane got a severe rap on the knuckles, but he took it on the chin.**

If you want to make comparisons, fine. They're often the spiciest parts of a piece of writing (to use a metaphor). But for as long as you're using the metaphor, be consistent. Avoid sentences like this, from a Geography essay:

**A virgin forest is one where the hand of man has never set foot.**

# Stating the Obvious

This is another part of the anti-clutter campaign. If readers can draw inferences, then there's no need to tell them. If you do, you've cluttered the sentence and the important things, although they're in there somewhere, are lost.

At the Seoul Olympics men's diving competition the hot favourite was the American, Greg Luganis. But, sensation! About to start one of his dives Luganis tripped and fell on the board. The commentator quickly told us:

**Luganis has accidentally hit his head on the board!**

Does this mean he normally does it deliberately?

It was hard to feel grateful to another commentator at the Olympics when he told us before the final of the men's 400-metre sprint that the Australian competitor, Darren Clark would 'try to run very well today'. Clark had been training for the race for four years: it was the biggest event of his career. We could have figured out all by ourselves that he'd be trying to run well.

# Confusion

There are times when you really wonder what people are trying to say. Consider this, from a tennis commentator:

**Chip Hooper is such a big man that it's sometimes difficult to see where he is on the court.**

What?

And from a UK sports commentator:

**A mediocre season for Nelson Piquet, as he is now known and always has been.**

Rod Marsh, discussing the Sri Lankan cricket team:

**They're still not without no chance.**

Does that mean they've got a chance, or not? I'm still trying to work it out. Rod's chalked up a triple negative. It takes a master to do that. The only other one I've heard was television presenter Don Lane on 'American Football' one night:

**'There's no way, I don't think, that that wasn't a fumble.'**

Sometimes it's not just confusion about English, it's confusion about Maths:

**I might be Scottish, but my ideas about the game are 360 degrees from the Scottish way. (Coach Eddie Thompson)**

**Queen's Park Oval, as the name suggests, is absolutely round. (Tony Cozier)**

**Initially leading 4 all, they're now a goal down again. (Television commentator on water polo)**

**Five years ago, when he was much, much younger ... (Bruce McAvaney)**

I thought we were all five years younger five years ago.

# Cliches

In everyday speech cliches are used a lot. People often don't have the mental energy to speak poetically or creatively or brilliantly – unless they're Oscar Wilde maybe, or Dorothy Parker. Cliches enable commonplace conversations to flow comfortably along:

'G'day, what do you know?'
'Not a lot. How are you?'
'Oh, fair to middling . . . Is that the baby?'
'Yeah, that's him.'
'Gee, there's no doubt who he takes after, hey!'

And so it goes on, a typical enough conversation that requires little effort for speaker or listener. When asked, 'Is that the baby?' only a smart alec would reply, 'No, it's a badly deformed pineapple'.

Cliches have their own conventions and rules, which are nearly always obeyed, although if we stopped and thought about what we were saying we'd often wonder. 'I'm going to grab forty winks', for example. This conjures up a bizarre image. 'They screamed blue murder.' What kind of murder is blue? 'I got off by the skin of my teeth.' It's interesting to think of teeth having skin, though the point of the phrase is of course that they have none.

Some cliches must have had great power when they were first used, because they were fresh and striking. 'I went like a bat out of Hell.' The picture of a small, black bat fleeing the fires of Hell is terrific. 'He was as thin as a rake.' Imagine that! And my grandmother's favourite: 'You'll be late for your own funeral'.

Nevertheless, cliches are usually best avoided in speech, and certainly best avoided in writing. If you speak or write in cliches, your audience will have only a shallow awareness of what you're saying: they'll be in a state of minimal involvement. It takes fresh language to grab attention, to hold interest.

Watching television soaps is interesting for a language student. Perhaps one reason for their popularity is that their scripts make few demands on the viewer. In a stressful world, people need little concentration to watch soaps. The scripts achieve this by endlessly using cliches. If you don't believe me, try watching a soap for five minutes and counting the number of cliches used. You should get at least fifteen or twenty. Here's five minutes of 'Days of Our Lives'.

**'It's no big deal.'**

**'I'm sorry about . . . '**

**'Hey, don't be. It's all going to change.'**

**'I could tell by the look in his eyes.'**

**'I can't be too choosy, the way things are going around here.'**

**'Most people don't care what people look like or the way they dress.'**

**'I have to do this – for me.'**

**'You and my dad have been through so much together.'**

**'I know how disappointed you must be.'**

**'It doesn't hold a torch to you – there's nothing in the world I'd trade for you.'**

**'We hardly spend any time alone.'**

**'So, what's it to be?'**

**'Diana, I'm not a kid. You don't have to pretend with me.'**

**'Well, I guess I can't fool you.'**

It's as though they have a computer programmed with a few

thousand cliches, and to generate each new script they just press a button, the computer links up two hundred phrases and snap! That's today's episode.

A colleague once gave me a list of statements by sporting commentators at the Seoul Olympics. The common factor was the phrase 'and that's what the Olympics are all about'. So on the first day we were told: 'The Olympic Games are all about the pursuit of excellence'. But the next day it was: 'That's what the Olympics are all about – upsets'. And a bit later: 'With his last throw he's snatched the gold away from him and that's what the Olympics are all about'. Soon after, we heard: 'Last place in the semi-final. Three times gold medallist, but that's what it's all about'. A few days later: '. . . beaten by a very superior girl on the day and that's what sport's all about'. Towards the end: 'It's great that we see everyone competing because that's what the Olympics are all about'. And at the closing ceremony: 'This is what the Olympics are all about. It's the athletes, the people who leave us with all the memories'.

## Obfuscation

I've talked of clutter already. The worst kind of clutter occurs when words are unnecessarily long, or when sentences go on for ever.

Australian author Ivan Southall, one of our best stylists, has trained himself to go back through his first draft, deleting ten words per page. That's a good discipline!

In the middle of World War II, Winston Churchill, with all the pressures of leadership weighing him down, told his subordinates that he would not read anything they gave him unless they reduced it to one side of one sheet of paper. That's a good discipline too.

The American army had a motto: KISS, which stood for 'Keep It Simple, Stupid!' As in warfare, so in writing. I suppose the word 'obfuscation' is itself an example of obfuscation. A word like 'waffle' might be better.

In Years 11 and 12 in particular a kind of madness often seizes students, when they feel they have to write long complex sentences, or to use the biggest words they know. A great writer, like F. Scott Fitzgerald, can do it:

> **Most of the confidences were unsought – frequently I have feigned sleep, pre-occupation, or a hostile levity when I realized by some unmistakable sign that an intimate revelation was quivering on the horizon; for the intimate revelations of young men, or at least the terms in which they express them are usually plagiaristic and marred by obvious suppressions.**

But when a lesser writer, or speaker, tries it . . . ouch:

> **Their hopes of avoiding the follow-on were exacerbated . . . (Greg Matthews, reviewing a cricket match)**

This is from a document sent out by the British Department of Education to clarify some instructions they'd circulated earlier. Imagine what the instructions were like before they were clarified!

> **Where a pupil is unable to complete a SAT due to his absence from school . . . if in the opinion of his head teacher he has not done enough work as aforesaid, the levels of attainment determined by the teacher assessment shall be the levels for the purpose of article 7 unless the local education authority (in the case of a pupil at a school which the authority maintains) or SEAC (in the case of a pupil at a grant-maintained school) disagree, in which case the levels of attainment shall be such as the local authority or SEAC determine by reference to the work the pupil has done on the SAT in question.**

Here's ex-Prime Minister of Australia, Bob Hawke:

**While society cannot provide employment for its members, the production/work/income nexus has to be abandoned as a justification for our present parsimony to the unemployed. An assumption cannot be used to justify making second-class citizens of those who are unfortunate enough to constitute the living proof of the inaccuracy of the assumption.**

I wonder if he himself knew what he was saying.

As a general rule, if someone needs to read the sentence twice to work out what it means, it's a bad sentence. Every time a reader stops to do that, the flow has been interrupted, and you've jeopardised your chances of 'carrying the reader away' with your eloquence.

Obfuscation madness spreads even to primary schools. After I took a workshop at a school some poor Grade 6 kid, who'd been given the job of thanking me, stood up and delivered this sentence, without pausing for breath:

**I'd like to thank you for providing us with this educational experience.**

I thought that my workshop had failed. At another primary school, a girl said to the audience:

**Please show your appreciation by acclamation.**

Most of the kids sat there looking puzzled. They didn't realise she was asking them to clap.

Well, I think that's why they didn't clap. They certainly didn't clap.

When meaning is obscured by poor language choice, that's bad! For me it's summed up by a typically great moment in that great television series 'Gilligan's Island', when the Skipper says despairingly, 'Oh Gilligan, how can I understand what you're thinking when I can't even understand what you're saying?'

# Euphemisms

Euphemisms are words or phrases used by people when they want something to sound better than they're afraid it is. Because euphemisms muffle and distort meanings, they are always *bad!*

Some common euphemisms are 'rest room' or 'comfort station' for lavatory, 'termination of employment' for getting the sack, 'detention centre' for prison, 'passed away' or 'expired' for dying.

My brother was working as a physiotherapist in a hospital, where he was treating an elderly lady named Mrs Hall. One day he arrived at her bedside to find no trace of his patient. 'Where's Mrs Hall?' he asked a passing nurse.

'Oh,' she said, 'she's gone to Calvary.'

My brother thought this was a Christian euphemism for death. He was shocked. 'But she seemed so well yesterday,' he exclaimed.

'Oh yes,' the nurse said, 'but we send all the old people to Calvary.'

It turned out that Calvary was the name of a convalescent home.

In 1889 Thomas Hardy wrote *Tess of the d'Urbervilles* in which an innocent village girl is seduced and shamefully treated by a wealthy young man, a distant relative. I was seventeen when I read the book, and it wasn't until I got to page 259 that I realised that Tess had lost her virginity to Alec d'Urberville. After a long search back through the book I found the steamy scene; it was on page 90. It had been treated so delicately that it was hard to realise what had happened:

**'Tess!' said d'Urberville.**

**There was no answer. The obscurity was now so great that he could see absolutely nothing but a pale nebulousness at his feet, which represented the white muslin figure he had left upon the dead leaves. Everything**

else was blackness alike. D'Urberville stooped; and heard a gentle regular breathing. He knelt and bent lower till her breath warmed his face, and in a moment his cheek was in contact with her. She was sleeping soundly and upon her eyelashes lingered tears.

Darkness and silence rushed everywhere around. Above them rose the primeval yews and oaks of the chase, in which there poised gentle roosting birds in their last nap; and about them stole the hopping rabbits and hares. But might some say, where was Tess's guardian angel? Where was the providence of her simple faith? Perhaps, like that other god of whom the ironical Tishbite spoke, he was talking, or he was pursuing or he was in a journey, or he was sleeping and not to be awakened.

Why it was that upon this beautiful feminine tissue, sensitive as gossamer, and practically blank as snow as yet, there should have been traced such a coarse pattern as it was doomed to receive; why so often the coarse appropriates the finer thus, the wrong man the woman, the wrong woman the man, many thousand years of analytical philosophy have failed to explain to our sense of order. One may, indeed, admit the possibility of a retribution lurking in the present catastrophe. Doubtless some of Tess d'Urberville's mailed ancestors rollicking home from a fray had dealt the same measure even more ruthlessly towards peasant girls of their time. But though to visit the sins of the fathers upon the children may be a morality good enough for divinities, it is scorned by average human nature; and it therefore does not mend the matter.

As Tess's own people down in those retreats are never tired of saying among each other in their fatalistic way: 'It was to be'. There lay the pity of it. An immeasurable social chasm was to divide our heroine's personality thereafter from that previous self of hers who stepped from her mother's door to try her fortune at a poultry farm.

Thus Hardy euphemistically describes the end of Tess's innocence. It's hardly the kind of stuff to attract an M or R rating, but Hardy, in a preface, defends himself against anyone who is offended by the book, or finds that he/she 'cannot endure' it.

The modern reader is likely to find the euphemisms unendurable, rather than the sex.

Plain direct language is best. Leon Uris, author of books such as *Exodus* and *Mita 18*, said: '... you cannot lie to your typewriter. Sooner or later you must reveal your true self in your pages'. Euphemisms are dishonest, obfuscatory and often the products of fear. Plain language can help writer and reader to confront what some people would prefer to avoid – such as the person, obviously a fan of euphemism, who wrote this letter to the London *Daily Mirror*.

**Your front page article about Africans being shot made me feel sick. Could not this kind of story be condensed and made more pleasant?**

As you read this book, you are probably becoming more aware of the language around you. By now it may have occurred to you that a lot of the words and phrases we use every day are quite unsatisfactory. Now let's move on to look at specific ways to improve writing. We'll look not just at language, but at structure, technique, theme and plot.

PART 2

# The
# Practitioner

# Going in Circles

Endings are often a problem for the writer. Sometimes the perfect ending writes itself in an easy and natural way, but this doesn't always happen. Most people have to work for their endings. And that work is important. It's a cruel thing to have a reader be drawn in further and further, only to be dumped at the critical moment.

On the other hand, stage entertainers – singers and comedians, for example – know you should always leave an audience wanting more. So it is with writing. It's better to have the reader close the book reluctantly, regretfully thinking, 'Oh, I wish it had gone on forever', than have them counting the number of pages left, wondering if it will ever finish. Don't bash the situation, or the characters, to death. Use a light touch as you approach the ending.

Some readers don't like my endings. 'Don't you know how to end a story?' a girl complained. I think all my books have endings. I stop when there's nothing left to say.

One time-honoured way of ending a story is literally with a death, or many deaths. Some of Shakespeare's plays litter the stage with so many corpses in the last scene or two that it must have been difficult for the surviving actors to clamber over the bodies. In the last act of *Hamlet*, for example, the King, the Queen, Hamlet, Ophelia, Laertes, Rosencrantz and Guildenstern all die and that's most of the cast.

For most writers there's a limit to how many people can be killed off in a story. And note also that it's unusual for a professional writer to end a book written in the first person with the death of the person telling the story, though students do this quite often in their writing (and teachers nearly always object when they do). The Czech writer Bohumil Hrabal does it in *Closely Watched Trains*, and in *The Horse's Mouth* by Joyce Carey, the protagonist seems to be on his way out as the book ends. *The Sweetshop Owner* by Graham Swift has only a few first-person sections, but we feel as though we are right inside the main character's mind, and he too appears to die at the end of the book.

So it can be done if you're a good enough writer.

Another type of ending is the winding-down, often reflective, style. The climax is over, the tumult and the shouting have died, and in the last section we're told, in a quiet, subdued way, of the consequences. It can be like the ending of some movies, where the names of the main characters are flashed on the screen, with a line telling us what later became of each:

**Roslyn Beach is now in Alaska, studying ice.**
**Miguel Santana fulfilled his ambition to become a travel**
**writer. Married with three children, he lives in Belgium.**
**Gabriella Pistoni was killed in a train crash in Sydney.**

Among movies which have used this technique are *All the President's Men*, *The Boys of Company C*, and *Animal House*.

If you were to do this in a story or book you'd probably flesh it out a bit more. The last couple of paragraphs of Victor Hugo's *Hunchback of Notre Dame* are an example of this technique. So is this, the penultimate paragraph of Henry Fielding's *Jonathon Wild*:

**As to all the other persons mentioned in this history in the**
**light of greatness, they had all the fate adapted to it,**
**being every one hanged by the neck save two, viz Miss**
**Theodosia Snap, who was transported to America, where**
**she was pretty well married, reformed, and made a good**
**wife; and the count, who recovered of the wound he had**
**received from the hermit and made his escape into**
**France, where he committed a robbery, was taken, and**
**broke on the wheel.**

That takes care of everyone very neatly.

The last chapter of *Middlemarch* by George Eliot, begins:

**All who have cared for Fred Vincy and Mary Garth will like to know that these two made no such failure, but achieved a solid mutual happiness ... Lydgate's hair never became white. He died when he was only fifty ... Sir James never ceased to regard Dorothea's second marriage as a mistake ...**

It's a seven-page summary of the outcomes for all the main characters.

Another common approach is to end the story with a few lines, paragraphs or pages in which a main character muses over what has happened, reflecting on what he/she has learned, or how he/she has changed. This often makes for a particularly pleasing ending. Examples abound.

*Lord of the Flies* by William Golding:

**And in the middle of them, with filthy body, matted hair, and unwiped nose, Ralph wept for the end of innocence, the darkness of man's heart, and the fall through the air of the true, wise friend called Piggy.**

*The Great Gatsby* by F. Scott Fitzgerald:

**And as I sat there brooding on the old unknown world, I thought of Gatsby's wonder when he first picked out the green light at the end of Daisy's dock. He had come a long way to this blue lawn, and his dream must have seemed so close that he could hardly fail to grasp it. He did not know that it was already behind him, somewhere back in the vast obscurity beyond the city, where the dark fields of the republic rolled on under the night.**

**Gatsby believed in the green light, the orgiastic future that year by year recedes before us. It eluded us then, but that's no matter – tomorrow we will run faster, stretch out our arms further ... And one fine morning –**

So we beat on, boats against the current, borne back ceaselessly into the past.

*Sherston's Progress* by Siegfried Sassoon:

It had been a long journey from that moment to this, when I write the last words of my book. And my last words shall be these – that it is only from the inmost silences of the heart that we know the world for what it is, and ourselves for what the world has made us.

It is this kind of ending that brings us to the title of this chapter, 'Going in circles'. If you're not sure how to end a story, try bringing it back to the starting point. It's very satisfying for the reader if a story is structured in a circular way. In *The Hobbit*, for example, Bilbo ends up back where he started, in Hobbiton. But – and this is the art of the writer – a great deal has changed. By showing us this, Tolkien beautifully concludes his lesson: risk taking and adventures are important; growth and wisdom don't come from crawling into a hole and staying there. Bilbo has learnt that friendship really matters, life is wonderful, and gold and jewels aren't so important after all. When we see him back at Hobbiton and compare his attitudes to those he had at the beginning of the book we understand this in the most complete way possible.

You probably remember lots of children's picture books which have the same structure – *Where the Wild Things Are* by Maurice Sendak, for example. The book starts with Max being sent to his room for being naughty. It ends with him still in his room but, having worked off his rage, he is now enjoying supper.

My favourite endings are the ones where I get a sense of life continuing: that the story is merely an important episode out of a life, but much has happened before the story begins and more will happen after it ends. This is from *My Childhood* by Maxim Gorky:

**A few days after Mother's funeral Grandfather said, 'Alexei, you're not a medal, you're only hanging around my neck. There's no room for you here. You must go out into the world!'**

**And so I went out into the world.**

In Mark Twain's *Huckleberry Finn,* one adventure ends, another begins:

**... so there ain't nothing more to write about, and I am rotten glad of it, because if I'd a-knowed what a trouble it was to make a book I wouldn't a-tackled it and ain't a going to no more. But I reckon I got to light out for the Territory ahead of the rest, because Aunt Sally she's going to adopt me and civilise me, and I can't stand it. I been there before.**

And in *Call of the Wild* by Jack London:

**But he is not always alone. When the long winter night come on and the wolves follow their meat into the lower valleys, he may be seen running at the head of the pack through the pale moonlight or glimmering borealis, leaping gigantic above his fellows, his great throat a-bellow as he sings a song of the younger world, which is the song of the pack.**

And, more overtly, in Wilkie Collins' *The Moonstone:*

**So the years pass and repeat each other; so the same events revolve in the cycles of time. What will be the next adventures of the Moonstone? Who can tell?**

Many books, of course, work in a 'time-line' manner. They start with an event which is followed by a series of other events in chronological order and the book ends when the last event (usually the most dramatic) takes place. There's a logic to it, a sense of progress, a sense of inevitability. It happens this way in most thrillers, horror stories and detective novels but also in many books that recount people's lives and relationships. At the end of the book, the final climax having occurred, there's a sense that it's all over and life can go back to normal.

*Pic* by Jack Kerouac:

**And Sheila run up, kissed his hungrianly, and we went in and eat the steak she saved up for us, with mashy potatoes, pole beans, and cherry banana spoon ice-cream split.**

Oliver Goldsmith's *The Vicar of Wakefield*:

**As soon as dinner was over, according to my old custom, I requested that the table might be taken away, to have the pleasure of seeing all my family assembled once more by a cheerful fireside. My two little ones sat upon each knee, the company by their partners. I had nothing now on this side of the grave to wish for; all my career were over; my pleasure was unspeakable. It now only remained that my gratitude in good fortune should exceed my former submission in adversity.**

They may sometimes get a little too sentimental for modern tastes, as in *Anne of Green Gables* by L. M. Montgomery:

**Anne's horizons had closed in since the night she had sat there after coming home from Queens, but if the path set before her feet was to be narrow she knew that flowers of quiet happiness would bloom along it. The joys of sincere work and worthy aspiration and congenial friendship were to be hers; nothing could rob her of her birthright of fancy or her ideal world of dreams. And there was always the bend in the road!**

**'God's in his Heaven, all's right with the world,' whispered Anne softly.**

At the end of Shakespeare's tragedy *Julius Caesar* the forces of Mark Antony have defeated the 'conspirators', Brutus and Cassius. Although Brutus dies during the battle he was much respected by his opponents, as the closing moments of the play confirm:

*Antony*: **This was the noblest Roman of them all.**
**All the conspirators save only he**
**Did that they did in envy of great Caesar;**
**He only, in a general honest thought**
**And common good to all, made one of them.**
**His life was gentle, and the elements**
**So mix'd in him that**
**Nature might stand up**
**And say to all the world,**
**'This was a man!'**

*Octavius*: **According to his virtue let us use him**
**With all respect and rites of burial.**
**Within my tent his bones tonight shall lie,**
**Most like a soldier, order'd honorably.**
**So, call the field to rest; and let's away;**
**To part the glories of this happy day.**

Perhaps my all-time favourite ending is from Harper Lee's *To Kill a Mockingbird*. It conveys beautifully the feeling that the drama is over and life will continue. 'He' is Atticus, Jem's father; Jem has just been sedated after breaking his arm:

**He turned out the light and went into Jem's room. He**
**would be there all night, and he would be there when Jem**
**waked up in the morning.**

Of course your endings don't have to be as conventional as these. You can go for the completely bizarre. Try this, from Henry Miller's *Sexus*:

'Woof! Woof! Woof woof!' I barked. 'Woof! Woof, woof, woof!'

The worst kind of endings are the dream ones – 'I felt my mother shaking my shoulder and woke up and realised it had all been a dream' – or the newspaper ones – 'DAILY NEWS: The body of a young girl was found at 28 Chichester Avenue yesterday. Police said she appeared to have taken her own life'.

These are stale, unimaginative and lazy ways to end a story.

## SUMMARY

♦ Leave the reader wanting more.

♦ Possible endings include death, a summary of what happened afterwards, a character reflecting on what she/he has learned, taking the story back to its starting point, a suggestion that further adventures await or a suggestion that it's all over and normal life can resume.

# Good for a Laugh

Every piece of writing is better for some humour.

I'm not sure whether I believe this myself, but I'd enthusiastically agree if the word 'long' was inserted between 'every' and 'piece'.

Alfred Hitchcock believed suspense and black comedy had to be used together to achieve the scariest possible effect in movies. In fact almost every successful film or book, in every genre, uses humour. But not just films and books. Most pieces of writing benefit from the inclusion of a few funnies: job applications, letters to bank managers, History essays.

Can you think of any film or book that you've liked that's had no humour in it? It's not easy. I can't think of any jokes in the Bible, but there may be a few somewhere. Shakespeare certainly understood the importance of humour, a clown or a fool is an obligatory cast-member of almost all his plays, even the tragedies. And some of Shakespeare's jokes are very rude indeed.

One of the suggestions that the editor made after reading the first draft of my novel, *So Much to Tell You*, was that it needed more humour. Hence I added a few lighter moments, like the birthday card that Marina remembers innocently making for her grandmother.

**A card! Huh! Last time I gave her a card I was about six or seven and I made it myself. Not knowing what to put on it, I went into the newsagent and memorised a message that was on a card in there. I can't remember now exactly what it was, but there was a chicken and an egg and some message about 'your birthday being a good time to get laid'. It didn't make much sense to me but I figured the adults would work it out. They did. That was the last time I made any birthday cards.**

What are the functions of humour? Well, humour gives the reader breathing space, time to regather before the book launches its next emotional assault. No one can put up with endless intensity – there have to be breaks. By putting off the climax a little longer humour can also make the climax more effective, by adding to the anticipation.

Humour can give a story or a character sweetness, so that the reader feels more warmth towards him/her. Conversely a humourless character can be particularly repellent to the reader – keep this in mind if you want to create someone truly unsympathetic in a story. One of the reasons George Orwell's *1984* is so horrifying is that the society it depicts is so humourless. In *Lord of the Flies* only Ralph has a sense of humour, but Golding writes of Piggy with humour on occasions, which helps us to like him. Charles Dickens created one of fiction's most unpleasant characters in the utterly humourless Uriah Heep in *David Copperfield*. Uriah laughs occasionally, but there's no warmth or humour in his laughter:

**Uriah stopped short, put his hands between his great knobs of knees, and doubled himself up with laughter. With perfectly silent laughter. Not a sound escaped from him. I was so repelled by his odious behaviour, particularly by this concluding instance, that I turned away without any ceremony; and left him doubled up in the middle of the garden, like a scarecrow in want of support.**

So, it's a powerful weapon, but of course forced humour doesn't work. Humour has to be used with a light touch. If you're writing a love story, a war story, a horror story or any dramatic or emotional piece, you may find that one humorous moment in the whole essay is just right. The same applies to non-fiction: in a piece of critical analysis or personal writing, one joke is often enough. But they're the moments that readers tend to remember most fondly and react to most favourably.

Even a grim book like *Wuthering Heights* by Emily Bronte has its moments. Mr Lockwood is trying to make conversation with Mrs Heathcliff and he proceeds by flattering her cat:

**'A beautiful animal!' I commented again. 'Do you intend parting with the little ones, Madam?'**
**'They're not mine,' said the amiable hostess more repellingly than Heathcliff himself could have replied.**
**'Ah, your favourites are among these,' I continued, turning to an obscure cushion full of something like cats.**
**'A strange choice of favourites,' she observed scornfully. Unluckily, it was a heap of dead rabbits.**

Now here's something else to think about: All humour contains elements of tragedy, and elements of cruelty. Is this true? If it is entirely or even partly true, does it help to explain why humour is so powerful for us?

## SUMMARY

♦ Use humour to give readers light relief or to give a character sweetness.

♦ To render a character odious, make him/her humourless.

# Sources for Stories

Stories come from only two places: experience and imagination.

Yes, it's that easy. Some stories – biographies, autobiographies, memoirs – come just from the first category, but all fiction comes from a combination of the two. Even the most exotic stories, which might at first seem products of the imagination, really draw on experiences as well. In writing *The Hobbit* and *Lord of the Rings*, J. R. R. Tolkien drew on his enormous knowledge of Anglo-Saxon, Finnish and Norse myths. When we look at Lewis Carroll and J. M. Barrie we understand how much their creations *Alice in Wonderland* and *Peter Pan* reflect their authors' lives.

Carroll was an eminent mathematician whose interest in logic can be seen in the crazy logical games in *Alice's Adventures in Wonderland*:

'Fourteenth of March, I think it was,' he said.
'Fifteenth,' said the March Hare.
'Sixteenth, said the Dormouse.
'Write that down,' the King said to the jury; and the jury eagerly wrote down all three dates on their slates, and then added them up, and reduced the answer to shillings and pence.

Barrie's tragic obsession with his brother, who died at age thirteen, strongly influenced his writing. Whilst Barrie had to grow up, his brother stayed thirteen forever, just like Peter Pan.

Experiences used in stories can be our own or other people's. They can be slight and momentary, or powerful, on-going and unforgettable.

Newspapers are among the best sources of stories about

other people's experiences. Among the ones I've cut out of newspapers over the years are these:

**A man in Bangkok who asked his parents for a motorbike when he was twenty locked himself in his room when they refused to give him one. At the age of forty-two he was still there, in the twenty-second year of his world-record sulk.**

**In Poland in 1991 three people were arrested with a metal detector on the site of a Nazi death camp, where 250,000 victims of the camp were buried. The three were hoping to steal jewellery from the buried bodies.**

**Also in 1991, an American couple deliberately had a second baby so that its marrow could be used for a transplant for their first daughter, who had leukaemia.**

**When, at the age of six, Prince William got involved in a scuffle with another little kid in a public swimming pool, a team of security men went into maximum alert, rushed over to them, separated them and whisked the prince straight back to his palace.**

**The American city of Dallas, hosting a Republican party political convention, rounded up all the tramps and homeless people in town and booked them into hotels at the city's expense, so that they wouldn't spoil the appearance of the streets.**

**A man in Queensland had a few drinks after a game of bowls, then left the club to drive three kilometres home. Somehow – he doesn't remember how – he drove 110 kilometres to a coal mine and kept driving 600 metres down a shaft. He was found there by miners as they**

started work the next morning. He was still sitting in his car.

Off the Indonesian coast a school of dolphins nudged and guided two shipwrecked sailors all night long until they reached an island and safety.

An American caught a plane that he thought was going to Oakland, California, but to his astonishment he found himself in Auckland, New Zealand. He'd misheard the flight call.

In Corsica a spectator at a soccer match saw the ball rolling towards his team's goal. He pulled out a gun and shot the ball, preventing the goal from being scored and bringing the match to a sudden end. He got three months' jail.

All these stories were presented as true by reputable newspapers. And they may all be true. But what does it matter if they are not? They're all bizarre, fascinating stories, in their own different ways. Though I haven't used any of them in novels, there are plenty of others that I have. My novels *So Much to Tell You* and *Letters from the Inside* were both partly inspired by newspaper stories: *So Much to Tell You* by the courage of Kay Nesbitt, who was disfigured after being shot in the face.

But newspapers alone aren't a sufficient source. The good writer is observant, and part of being observant is to notice the big and little stories happening around us all the time, in our own lives even. Schools are always full of stories. I once worked in a school where a boy had died from illness at the age of fourteen. This was a sad and terrible thing. Later they held a memorial service for him at the school. Two of his friends arrived for the service but were sent away by a teacher because they weren't wearing school uniform. This too was sad and terrible.

A boy I taught told me about his sister, who was born with severe mental disabilities. From infancy this girl had been looked after by her grandmother, in a distant suburb, with the result that the brother and sister barely knew each other.

In a boarding school where I worked I liked the way two Year 7 girls pretended that the shape of leaves from a tree pressing on their window was a face. They called it Max and it became a running story in their lives. They alternated between being scared of their own creation and laughing at themselves for their fears. I used Max in the book *Out of Time*.

Little stories and big stories. Don't just look out for the great dramatic events: the wars, the passionate romances, the heroic struggles, the bomb blasts. You may need those to help give backbone to a piece of writing, but you'll certainly need the little stories too. Some writers, such as Anne Tyler, write wonderful books which detail the everyday events in the lives of ordinary people. I collect little stories because I need them in my novels to add colour and depth, to fill in background, to improve credibility. For instance, a girl called Anna, who arrived for her first day in secondary school with her fingernails all painted different colours, gave me an incident I used to help create the character of Melanie in *The Great Gatenby*. In her first appearance in the book I wanted Melanie to establish herself as spirited, colourful, wild:

'Secondly,' he went on, 'I notice one of the girls has different colour nail polish on each of her fingers. That is not the way we do things here at Linley.'

Everyone gazed at the girl, who was sitting on the arm of a chair in the middle of the room. Her parents were red with humiliation. The girl stared right back at the

**Housemaster. I fell in love with her on the spot.**

**'What's wrong with different coloured nail polish?' she asked. The room trembled. I was too scared to be in love with her any more.**

**The Housemaster, whose normal colour was green, turned a sort of volcanic grey. It was a crucial moment for him – lose it now and he'd lost it forever.**

**'That's one of the rules we have here,' he said at last. He'd lost it.**

I remember 'collecting' another story about fingernails: one day I ran into a girl who'd just come from a French class, where she'd entertained herself by painting her nails with liquid paper, then decorating each one with different tricolour designs, red, white and blue. Little stories can be like that: a moment, a quick image, a glimpse. Another from my notebook is that of the boy who went one day to splatter a fly on a window with his hand. He hit too hard, killed the fly, but broke the window as well.

My own most memorable experience with a fly came when I was addressing an audience in a hall in Melbourne. Everybody spits occasionally as they talk, and I'm no exception. Halfway through a sentence in my speech a drop of spit flew out of my mouth and shot down a blowfly that happened to be passing at the time. I was so amazed that I couldn't go on with my talk. I stood there gaping at the fly, thinking: 'If I practised for ten years I'd never get off a shot as good as that again'. Meanwhile, the fly was sprawled on the table in front of me, looking puzzled, and slightly shocked. The audience was too far away to see any of this: they couldn't understand why I'd stopped speaking and was gazing at the desk. After a few seconds I gathered myself together and continued with the speech. But I've never forgotten that fly.

Not long ago I was in an expensive, upmarket shoe shop in Melbourne. Not the kind of shop I'm normally found in, but I'd gone there on impulse. And I was going through the usual routines when one tries on new shoes. You know how it is: you put on one, or both, then go for a test drive, a lap or two of the store. I was doing that, and glancing down at the shoes to admire them, when suddenly I noticed a big swelling in the leg of my jeans, below the left knee. What could it be? Allergy to shoes? Cancer? I balanced on one foot and tried to look up my own leg, not easy when you're wearing jeans. And finally I realised. The night before, I'd taken off my jeans and jocks in one movement, the way you do. This morning I'd put on clean jocks, then yesterday's jeans. But yesterday's jocks were still in the leg of the jeans! And what was worse, they were slipping down a few centimetres with every step I took. In another half dozen steps my underwear would be sitting on the thick carpet of the shop. What could I do? Only the obvious thing: I ducked behind a rack of shoes and started groping up my own leg; again not easy when you're wearing jeans. Finally I made contact and pulled them out, and stuffed them quickly in my pocket. But as I did, I looked up. The woman selling me the shoes was craning her neck from behind the counter, trying to make out what I was doing. I don't know whether she thought I was a shoplifter, or some kind of pervert who liked to wave his underwear around in shoe shops.

It was six months before I could even smile about that experience; it was too humiliating. But eventually I came to see its funny side.

Not all stories happening around us are humorous. Friends of mine had a friend who was a judge. The time came when the judge discovered he had cancer, and could expect to live only a short time. My friends were talking to him one night.

**'Have you enjoyed your career in law?' they asked him.**

**'No,' he answered fiercely, 'I've hated every minute of it.'**

They were astonished. 'But what would you rather have done?'

The Judge replied, 'Medicine. For as long as I can remember I've wanted to be a doctor.'

'Well, why didn't you do medicine?'

'Because my mother wanted me to, and there was no way I was going to give her the satisfaction.'

It's hard to explain why different stories attract people. And of course a story that works for one person may not work for another – it depends on things like personality and interests. But it's possible to identify at least two factors that often play a part:

1. Stories that involve strong feelings always seem to have power. In the last two anecdotes quoted above, strong feelings are certainly present: embarrassment in the first, hatred and bitterness in the second. Any time you want to create a strong piece of writing, start with a situation where strong passions are involved. Your starting point may be an experience of your own. Think of a time when you were gripped by intense feelings: a time when you were particularly proud of something you'd achieved, a time when you were jealous of someone else, a time when you felt great compassion, a time when you loved or hated. A piece of writing that does nothing else but describe such an experience will nearly always work (though of course it will be non-fiction).

Someone once gave me a list of human emotions ranging from elation to fear, from desire to anger to empathy. There were 140 different emotions on the list, so it should be a while before you run out of topics to write about.

2. Stories that involve a change in status or a battle for status are powerful, too. If you look back through the anecdotes I've used in this section you'll find status struggles are an element of most of them. Take a simple example: the boy who goes to squash the fly on the window. As he goes to squash it he has very high status. He is big and strong (in

relation to the fly) and he is acting assertively, powerfully. As he splatters the fly he's a miniature Arnold Schwarzenegger. But an instant later, when the window breaks, he's reduced to a klutz, a clumsy person. His status suddenly drops to about the level of the fly, which is very low indeed. Dead flies have rarely enjoyed much status in our culture (or in any other).

Why is it that change-of-status stories are fascinating to us humans? We'll have a longer look at status later.

# More Sources

## Animal Stories

Most people seem to have good animal stories to tell. Anyone who's owned or observed a dog, cat, horse, Tasmanian tiger or other living creature can write at least one piece about these animals, and it'll usually make good reading. A boy called Rhys had a story I liked about his dog. It seems that the day came when the dog had to go to the vet, so Rhys's mother put it on the passenger seat of the car, looped the end of the lead over the top of the seat, wound the window lower to give the dog air, and set off down the road.

As people do, she slipped into 'automatic pilot' mode once she reached the freeway and drove along with the radio on, gazing at the traffic. It was some kilometres before she thought to look across to see how the dog was going. When she did, she was horrified to see that the dog was gone! The lead was still looped around the top of the seat, but there was no dog!

So Rhys' mother did the obvious thing and looked in the wing-mirror. And there was the dog, being towed along in the slipstream at a hundred kilometres an hour, the lead still fastened to its collar. Naturally she braked instantly, jumped out and rescued the dog. According to Rhys it had come to no harm, and still reacts with enthusiasm every time it's given a chance to go for a ride in the car. Maybe the dog really enjoyed the experience – maybe it was like hang-gliding, or water-skiing. Or maybe they've just got a very stupid dog.

# Injuries

As well as animal stories, people often have a fund of stories to do with injuries and illnesses. Being hurt, or coming close to being hurt, is an experience that we don't quickly forget. Falling off bicycles or motorbikes or skateboards or horses or surfboards, falling out of trees, being in car accidents, cutting oneself, breaking bones, shedding blood: the person who has no stories like these is rare indeed, and is probably living too cautiously.

# Death

Another important source of stories is death. It would be almost impossible to write a true story about death and make that story boring, or a failure. Death has such power for us: we read about it, remember our dealings with it, reflect on its meaning. If I had to nominate the closest an Australian writer has come to perfection, I'd choose Tom Collins' account of the death of a little girl who'd been lost in the bush. It comes half-way through Chapter Eight of his book *Such is Life*.

**Poor Dan! He walked behind the wagonette all the way, crying softly, like a child, and never taking his eyes from the little shape under the soaking wet blanket. Hard lines for him! He had heard her voice calling him, not an hour before; and now, if he lived till he was a hundred, he would never hear it again.**

It's not just the death of humans, but the death of animals that is worth recording. A. B. Facey's 'Killing the Pig' in *A Fortunate Life* is a classic of Australian bush life. The death of any pet, from a guinea pig to a goldfish, can be told to great effect even by an inexperienced writer. And the mood need not be sombre. Each person approaches each death differently.

# How to Use Experiences

We have all had thousands of experiences, at first hand, or second, or twentieth. The question is, how to use them in a piece of writing?

This isn't so difficult for the average-length class assignment. The rule is, if the story's good enough, let it tell itself. Take one experience and write it out from start to finish, imagining that you're recounting it to a friend. You can't go wrong doing that. If you want a more sophisticated approach then there's plenty of suggestions in this book for you to think about.

For a longer work of fiction things may be more complicated. Many novels have two or three 'long' stories and perhaps hundreds of little ones, all intermeshed. Harper Lee's *To Kill a Mockingbird* is the story of the Finch family during a dramatic period of their lives, but it is also the story of the persecution and death of Tom Robinson. And it is the story of the sad life of Boo Radley. These three big stories cross and recross each other on almost every page of the book. Then there are the little stories: the childhood of Dill, the curious life of Mr Dolphus Raymond, the half-hearted courtship of Miss Maudie by Uncle Jack Finch, the struggles of Miss Caroline Fisher in her first teaching assignment, the lonely death of Mrs Dubose. It would be an interesting exercise (well, I think it would) to rank the hundreds of stories in *To Kill a Mockingbird* in order of importance, from the persecution of Tom Robinson (is that the most important one?) down to, say, the life of Cousin Ike Finch.

If you don't remember Cousin Ike it's not surprising. He

occupies only one paragraph in the whole novel. But it's those little stories as much as the big ones that ensure the success of the whole structure. The individual bricks in a building are as important as the foundation and the framework.

When I wrote *Letters from the Inside* I used two main stories, the lives of its two protagonists, Tracey and Mandy. The book came about in the following way: it began with a conversation with a girl who was seventeen and just finishing boarding school. When I innocently suggested that she must be happy to leave school and have some time at home she contradicted me. She told a chilling story about her brother, who was so violent that he sounded almost psychopathic. She was terrified to be alone with him. I was shocked by her story, and could not get it out of my mind.

Later I read a newspaper story about a girl who'd been taken suddenly from her home to live with her grandmother. A long time later she was told that her mother had died and her father had 'gone away'. It wasn't until she was in her mid-teens that she accidentally found out the truth: her father had murdered her mother and been sent to jail for it. This story also made a great impact on me and it too stayed in my memory.

At the same time I was thinking a lot about the fantasies people create about themselves and their lives; the way they lie to themselves and to others when they're not satisfied with the lives they're leading. (Do we all do that?)

Add to that my fascination with institutions, places where people are held together in close proximity, like hospitals, jails, schools (especially boarding schools) – and the major elements of *Letters from the Inside* can all be recognised.

The next step was to let these elements and others ferment in my mind. I was content to let my subconscious do the work. For some months, as I worked in my garden or drove around the state or walked the dog, I let the different stories and ideas insinuate themselves through and around each other. One day, in the garden (I can even point out the exact spot where I was standing) a structure emerged which incorporated most of what I wanted. Other ideas which would not be used in the book fell away, and I knew the story was ready to be told. I laid down my fork, went inside, and began writing.

A final word though: don't forget those little stories! They're often what give the completed work its colour, its richness. They can be as important as the main plots.

## SUMMARY

♦ Be observant.
♦ Collect big and little stories.
♦ Find stories of passion.
♦ Find stories of status.
♦ Stories of animals, illness and death can be powerful.

# Imagination

Not just in writing, but in everything, imagination is a vital essence that gives life.

A few years ago, Greg Norman, ranked the number one golfer in the world, had a shot that looked impossible. A rock between his ball and the hole blocked his approach completely. There seemed no solution that would keep him in a competitive position in the tournament. Norman astonished everybody. He turned his back on the hole and hit the ball in the opposite direction, because he had seen what others had not: that he could bounce the ball off a second rock away to the side, and ricochet it towards the hole, like a pool shot.

The television commentators were in awe and so was I. 'That,' one of them proclaimed, 'simply requires great imagination.'

When a new coach, Terry Wheeler, took over the Western Bulldogs football team, he had remarkable success. Halfway through the season, the *Age* newspaper ran an article about him, discussing and analysing his achievements. The article included this sentence: 'Part of what Terry Wheeler is appealing to in his young team is its imagination'.

Yes, that word again. It seems that at the top level of professional sport imagination is recognised as one of the keys to success.

Writer John Berger, in an essay called 'A Fortunate Man', explored the life, career and philosophy of a doctor named John Sassall. It's evident to the reader that Sassall is indeed a fortunate man, deeply interested in his work and deeply interesting. Berger describes Sassall's evolution from a doctor of limited vision to one of remarkable breadth of outlook thus: 'He began to realise that he must face his imagination, even explore it ... he began to realise that imagination had to be lived with on every level: his own imagination first, because otherwise this could distort his observation, and then the imagination of his patients.'

It doesn't matter what your ambitions are. Perhaps you want to be a sports professional, perhaps a doctor, a farmer, a hairdresser, a cook, a teacher or a gardener. Can you imagine how boring these jobs would be, and how limited your success, if you approached them without imagination? Can you name anyone who has reached the top in any field and has got there without using imagination?

It is to be hoped, though, that your ambitions extend a little more widely than this. Among the worthiest ambitions in our society are to be a good friend, a good partner in a loving relationship and a good parent perhaps. Again, the more imagination you bring to these challenges, the more successful you will be, and the better other people will respond to you.

In writing, what exactly is imagination? We use the word frequently as though we assume everybody means the same thing by it.

Here's one aspect of it: imagination includes the ability to leave your mind and go into something else, most commonly the mind of another person. The reason I don't bother with drugs is that I know that I can do as much or more with my imagination as other people do with drugs. Also I value my imagination and know that some drugs would actually alter or damage it. I'm not keen on that prospect.

'To go into something else ... ' It's as though you become the other person. You do it by practice and concentration. Lots of people use meditation, but I'm not that organised about it. But with imagination you can think yourself into another person or thing, another place, another time. You can write convincingly from the perspective of an eight-year-old in sixteenth-century France, a drug-dealer in contemporary Tokyo, a grandmother in Zimbabwe in 2050.

(Not forgetting, of course, that factual knowledge may be needed in conjunction with imagination, and research may be needed to supply that.)

Once you've thought yourself there, you can write convincingly. How else could Anna Sewell have become a horse in *Black Beauty*, David Malouf, a Roman poet who lived two thousand years ago in *An Imaginary Life* or Paul Jennings, a boy with a seven-centimetre nose in 'The Gum Leaf War'?

### SUMMARY

♦ Imagination will enrich your life literally and metaphorically.

♦ To write fiction convincingly you need an 'out-of-body experience', imagining yourself into your character's skin.

# Using Language to Good Effect

Is there such a thing as a bad sentence? How about this?

**My heart shattered and I wept bitter sobs.**

Yes, it's a terrible sentence. But why? Go back to the sentence and note the number of 'strong' words in it. There's at least four: shattered, wept, bitter, sobs. Possibly heart as well. This is why the sentence fails. It's groaning under the weight of too many strong words.

In English, as in all languages presumably, there are many powerful words. These words cannot be crowded together. They must be given a lot of space, room to breathe. Otherwise, like roosters in a cage, they'll peck each other to death.

Here is the shortest verse in the Bible. Is it a good sentence?

**Jesus wept.**

The word 'wept', a strong word, is allowed room to have its effect.

Nearly everybody who writes in English overwrites. It's usually because they want to make maximum impact. They feel that a sentence like 'I was frightened' or 'He wept' will not make enough impression on the reader.

In 1984 the Australian War Memorial published *Australians at War*, a selection of photographs of Australian servicemen and women, spanning eighty-seven years. The editors of this volume had over 500,000 prints to choose from. They chose 200 or so but they didn't give in to the temptation to cram photos into every spare centimetre of every page. There is one photograph to each page and on some pages the amount of white space exceeds the size of the picture.

As with photos, so with words. 'Less is more' is an important paradox of language. Few strong words: one per sentence, one or two per paragraph, four to six per essay, will normally be about right. Reserve them for times of greatest need. Chekhov said, 'When you want to touch the reader's heart, try to be colder.' He practised what he preached, too. Here he writes of the death of love and youth, and life itself, in his character, a woman named only as Miss N.N. When she was young a man called Peter Sergeich had expressed his love for her, one wild, passionate evening. Nothing, however, came of the affair:

My father died. I have grown old. All that pleased me, that caressed me, that gave me hope – the noise of rain, the rolling of thunder, the thoughts of happiness, the words of love – all this has become a mere recollection, and I see before me a flat, empty plain; there is not a single living soul on the plain, and there on the distant horizon it is dark and terrible ...

There was a bell. Peter Sergeich had come to see me. When I see the country in winter and remember how green it became for me in summer, I whisper: 'Oh, my darlings!'

And when I see the people with whom I passed my spring, I grow sad and warm, and I whisper the same words.

Long since, by my father's influence, he had been transferred to town. He has grown somewhat older, somewhat thinner. Long ago he ceased to talk to me of love, he no longer talked nonsense, he did not like his work; he had some sort of ailment, he was disappointed with something; he had given up expecting anything from life and he had no zest in existence. He sat down near the fire and looked silently into the flames.

The poignancy of her situation, the desolation of her life, are expressed with restraint. The writer has not taken up all the emotional space available: he has left room for us to empathise with Miss N.N.'s empty existence.

If I'm proud of any sentence in my own books it's this two-word one, from *Letters from the Inside.* 'Three stars.' It occurs in a paragraph when Tracey is describing the view from her cell. I wanted to give an image of how sad her situation was, that she could only see a tiny patch of sky. Also, I wanted to show a facet of her personality that she herself was trying to conceal. She wants to be tough but we know by the fact that she was aware of these stars and counted them, that they were important to her. We can assume she does have a sensitive side, if we didn't already know that.

Another way people damage words is to use qualifiers. As if the words aren't strong enough already, they add a few more to shore them up, although most words can work on their own anyway. In trying to strengthen other words, the qualifiers often weaken them. Words like just, very, quite, really, absolutely, arguably, tremendously, extremely could be scrapped from the English language without being much missed. As the 'Wizard of Id' comic strip once asked, 'What *is* so pretty about soon?'

**It was just about to rain.**

**It was about to rain.**

Is there a difference in meaning? If not, less is better. Use the second sentence.

**We were really tired.**

**We were tired.**

At first glance the first one may seem stronger, but I'd suggest that the stark simplicity of the second, like a granite tor, is more effective.

**It was absolutely the worst moment of my life.**

**It was the worst moment of my life.**

This example is not so clear-cut. The first sentence is more emphatic. There are no rules in writing. It may suit some styles to use modifiers. It's probably true that all modifiers can be used to good effect occasionally; as in *Emma* by Jane Austen:

**He is undoubtedly very much in love – everything denotes it – very much in love indeed!**

Similarly, although I quoted 'less is more' as a dictum on the previous page I've heard of an architect who went on record as saying that 'less is a bore'. All writers have to find their own voice, their own style. But never underestimate the power of words. If you think of our language as a continuum then it might be clearer; for example:

freezing  chilled  cold  cool  tepid  warm  hot  boiling
└────────┴────────┴────────┴────────┴────────┴────────┴────────┘

Once we see that 'boiling' is at the extreme of the language then we see that there's no point adding modifiers to it. To say 'it was really boiling' or 'I'm absolutely boiling' does nothing because nothing can be done to 'boiling'. It's already at the limit! It cannot be strengthened.

good                                                        evil
└──────────────────────────────────────────────────────────┘

If evil isn't at the limit it's so close it doesn't matter.

Try placing other words across the spectrum.

enormous

ancient

perfect

revolting                                                    delicious

Here are some editing challenges from my own books,
mostly from *Burning For Revenge*. In each case I've indicated
in brackets the number of words I was able to cut from the
sentence. (Sometimes I had to put in a new word. The
number in brackets represents the net reduction.)

**They'll be able to hear you in Wirrawee. (3)**

**All I needed was to see a glimpse. (2)**

**I fired once and hit it, when the jeep was just ten metres
away from it. (2)**

**I scooped up the thousand pieces, marched down to the
gully and ceremoniously dumped the whole lot in there. (3)**

**Leaving the pack there I went forward ten metres and
turned on the torch. (1)**

**People write for a lot of reasons. (2)**

**'I don't see the big harm in picking it up,' Fi said. (2)**

**I had to be content with that, because there was no other
way to explain it. (2)**

**During each of these interruptions we hid in the same truck. (2)**

**Did you find any? (2)**

One of George Orwell's famous rules was: 'If you can cut a word out, cut it out.' I regard that as the best advice ever offered for writers.

Fifteen years ago I heard a wise headmaster remark that we 'are constantly weakening our most powerful words by sending them on petty missions'. It was a true thought, gracefully expressed. If you can appreciate the power of strong words you're starting to come to grips with our fascinating, beautiful language.

## SUMMARY

♦ Use strong words sparingly – less is more.

♦ Minimise your use of qualifiers.

♦ Recognise words that are at the limits already. There's nothing you can do to strengthen them.

# More on Style

Be a stingy writer! No matter how warm and generous you are in real life, develop a mean streak when you write. Sure, you have to be 'giving' in some ways, like taking risks and exposing yourself, but don't seek to hand the reader everything he/she wants. We know readers want to be moved, amused, stimulated, entertained, challenged and so on but if we try to do all this they won't be grateful. Be grudging, hand out small doses, make them wait, don't give them everything. The more intense the scene you're writing, the more true this is.

Think of the great books you've studied in English, the books you've learned to love and respect. Well, OK then, think of the books your English teacher loves and respects, even if you don't. In *My Brilliant Career* by Miles Franklin we want Sybylla to marry Harry; we want it badly, but it's a better book because she doesn't. In William Golding's *Lord of the Flies* we want Ralph and Piggy to triumph over Jack and Roger and the forces of evil – well, unless we're really sick we do – but how much more powerful is their failure? *Animal Farm* and *1984* by George Orwell, *The Chocolate War* by Robert Cormier, *The Pigman* by Paul Zindel and Shakespeare's *Romeo and Juliet* and *Hamlet* are all commonly studied in schools. In all of them we see the destruction of people we like, people we sympathise with – even as we long for their happiness.

When I finally got around to watching a modern horror movie I was disappointed. Expecting to be frightened and disgusted, I was faintly amused and a little bored. (The movie was *Nightmare on Elm Street II* I think.) The director should have been stingier with the horror, shown more restraint. A more effective film is the 1948 black-and-white version of *Oliver Twist*. In one scene Bill Sikes is about to batter Nancy to death in her cheap little room. Many directors at this point would show close-ups of the hammer, the blood, Nancy's face, the whole works. But director David Lean, in consecutive images, induces true horror in his audience. We see Bill pick up a wooden club and advance on the terrified Nancy. Then the film cuts to Bill's dog. In a frenzy of fear, Bill's loyal bull terrier flings himself repeatedly at the door, trying to escape. Bill's crime is so horrific that even his dog is scared of him, can't stand to be in the same room. We hear the thuds of the club, before the film jumps a few hours, to the onset of dawn. Bill and the dog are still in the room, but the dog now looks at Bill reproachfully. As soon as the door is opened the dog runs, shrieking, from the monster to whom he was once devoted.

Lean could have weakly given in to the cheapest tastes of his audience and indulged himself and them with litres of blood. By denying himself that path he has forced himself to be more creative. The result is one of the most disturbing episodes that I have seen in a cinema.

In well-written books, even when the good guys win, their triumph is often not unmitigated. Virtue triumphs in *Macbeth* but so many good people have died and so much damage has been done that we cannot rejoice. Virtue triumphs in *Hamlet*, but Hamlet and Ophelia are both dead. Mr Harding does the honourable thing in Anthony Trollope's *The Warden* but the hospital over which he presided degenerates, and its inmates suffer greatly.

Some modern examples are: the artistic triumph of Asher Lev in *My Name Is Asher Lev* by Chaim Potok, achieved at the cost of his relationship with his parents; the reunion with parents in *The Silver Sword* by Ian Serraillier, which comes only after the sacrifice of the dog, Ludwig, and is followed by emotional illness for some of the children; and the birth of the baby girl, Dusky, in *A Kindness* by Cynthia Rylant, which heals one relationship but ends another.

The grief, the love, the excitement – the feelings we

readers have – crave release and we want the writer to let them flood onto the page on our behalf. By not doing that, by not expressing them for us, the writer allows us room to feel them ourselves. We need that room. The more the writer allows our feelings to build up, the more intense will be whatever release we're finally allowed.

Here are three good rules for writing: understate, understate, understate. One has to be stingy with language, too, as discussed in the last section. Julia Macrae, an Australian who's now one of Britain's top publishers, has many manuscripts arriving on her desk each week for assessment. To decide which are worth close study she has a number of tests. One of them is to open the book somewhere in the middle and look for a passage of dialogue. When she finds dialogue she looks at the words used to describe the characters' speech. A passage like this indicates that the manuscript is in trouble already:

'That's right!' he laughed.
'The green ones too?' she queried.
'Yes,' he responded. 'Even them.'
'Well!' she exclaimed. 'I totally disagree.'

But a passage like this has passed Julia Macrae's first test:

'That's right!' he said.
'The green ones too?' she asked.
'Yes,' he said. 'Even them.'
'Well!' she said. 'I totally disagree.'

The second writer understands that the plain word 'said' is nearly always the most effective. You need only look at American short-story writer Raymond Carver or Australia's Paul Jennings to see the second style in action.

Many writers wallow in adjectives:

**It was a beautiful blue sunny day, and the shimmering sparkling water danced in the glorious sun's radiant rays.**

Don't laugh! You wouldn't if you'd marked as many English essays as I have. Students who write that way have probably been badly taught.

A lot of it comes down to trying too hard for an effect. I think this opening sentence of a novel by Thomas Pynchon is trying too hard, but not everyone would agree:

**Later than usual one summer morning in 1984, Lloyd Wheeler drifted awake in sunlight through a creeping fig that hung in the window, with a squadron of bluejays stomping on the roof.**

I get the feeling that Pynchon is admiring his own cleverness as he writes the last phrase. He'd have done better to stop at 'window'.

I prefer this awakening:

**The dog woke me by jumping on the bed and licking my face. When he got his tongue in my mouth I thought it was time to get up.**

If you want an example of try-hard writing at its worst, try this, from a newspaper advertisement for a dating agency:

**As she watched his face in the shimmer of morning sun, he tucked the wisp of hair behind her ear. Words tumble like a cool pebble brook, eyes laugh, hands touch. The day drifts away like the whisper of a summer breeze. That's two. We understand. Call us at . . .**

No, you can't leave the room. Try to fix your mind on something else. Tapeworms for example.

Another aspect of style is the use of repetition. Surely all writers use it to enhance their work:

**Cannon to right of them
Cannon to left of them
Cannon in front of them
Volleyed and thundered;**

**Stormed at with shot and shell,**
**Rode the six hundred.**
**Boldly they rode and well,**
**Into the Jaws of Death**
**Into the Mouth of Hell . . .**

Thus the fatal charge of the Light Brigade in the Crimean War, described by Tennyson.

Repetition can be effective, but like everything, must be used with careful judgement. Don't go to the well too often. Not too much repetition of repetition. Martin Luther King got it right – try listening to his famous speech at the Washington Monument.

One of the 'tricks' when using repetition is to vary the repetition, if that's not a contradiction in terms. Just when the reader is lulled into certainty about what's coming next – which is usually an undesirable situation – vary the pattern you've been using. For example:

**'You want to go for a walk?'**
**'No.'**
**'You want to watch a video?'**
**'No.'**
**'The beach?'**
**'No.'**
**'You want to go see Robert?'**
**'No, NEVER! I never want to see him again.'**

Just when we're expecting another 'No' we're jolted out of our complacency by a more emphatic statement.

# Show, Don't Tell

If you faithfully participated in 'Show-and-Tell' sessions at Primary School for years this heading might come as a shock.

'Show, don't tell' is a simple way of urging you to convey information to your reader with subtlety. Only the naive writer hands over everything packaged and ready to go. Far better to indicate the important things by delicate placement, allowing people to read between the lines. Consider this:

**I was walking down the beach at Port Whitehead one day. My name's Lucy and I'm 14 and I was staying there with my family – Mum, Dad and my two brothers – like we do every year. On this particular day it was raining but I wanted to go see my friend Jo who lives ...**

This is boring because there's nothing for the reader to do. The writer has told us everything. We might as well watch television. Contrast it with this:

**The phone rang.**
**'Bron?'**
**'Yes, Paul?'**
**'It's the mare. She's down again. Can you come out?'**
**'Is she distressed?'**
**'No – the opposite. Doc, can you come quickly?'**

I'm cheating a bit because this seems to be a more interesting situation than the first example. But it's also interesting because we don't know much yet. Human beings possess great curiosity. We'll keep reading to find out who these people are and what's going on. Yet we already know quite a lot and that's the beauty of this approach. We find out for ourselves (well, we think we do). Here we already know that the person telling the story is a vet named Bron, working with horses, on quite friendly terms (they use first names and she recognises his voice straight away) but not too friendly (he calls her 'Doc' at one stage) with a man called Paul.

Adverbs should not be used too often, as they often tell instead of show. To make it worse they're often tautologous.

**'You get out of my sight this instant,' he shouted angrily.**

No need to tell us he's angry; you've already shown us.

**'I love you,' he sighed romantically.**

A challenging exercise is to see how many facts you can convey without telling the reader directly. Try writing an opening to a story in which you subtly let the reader know the following details:

> It's winter, 1942; Sydney, Australia; the main character in your story is a newspaper vendor aged about sixteen who has a brother and a sister in the armed forces.

Or:

> It's 2050, in Africa, and your main characters are two prisoners in an old jail block. They're a married couple with strong religious beliefs. The woman is pregnant.

Or:

> A contemporary story in an overseas city of your choice. Your main character is a divorced police officer with a child. The child has just been caught shoplifting. The police officer's chief interests are swimming, music and old movies.

Here's how a professional writer does it. Margaret Atwood, beginning *The Handmaid's Tale*:

**We slept in what had once been the gymnasium. The floor was of varnished wood, with stripes and circles painted on it, for the games that were formerly played there; the hoops for the basketball nets were still in place, though the nets were gone. A balcony ran around the room, for the spectators, and I thought I could smell, faintly like an after image, the pungent scent of sweat, shot through with the sweet taint of chewing gum and perfume from the watching girls, felt-skirted as I knew from pictures, later in mini-skirts, then pants, then in one earring, spiky green streaked hair.**

**Dances would have been held there; the music lingered, a palimpsest of unheard sound, style upon style, an undercurrent of drums, a farborn wail, garlands made of tissue-paper flowers, cardboard devils, a revolving ball of mirrors, powdering the dancers with a snow of light.**

All good openings raise more questions than they answer; it is too early for Atwood to start answering questions, but her opening gives a wonderful sense of time passing, especially in her description of the changing styles of the girls who once played basketball in the gymnasium. We understand already that the story is set in the future and the narrator is sensitive and observant.

Mind you, many writers do begin with a direct account of what has led to the 'present' situation; as does Leo Tolstoy in *Anna Karenina*:

**Happy families are all alike; every unhappy family is unhappy in its own way.**

**Everything at the Oblonsky's was topsyturvy. Oblonsky's wife had found out that he had been having an affair with the French governess who used to live with them, and told him she could no longer stay under the same roof with him. This was the third day things had been this way, and not only the married couple themselves, but the family and the whole household were painfully aware of it. Everyone in the house felt that there was no sense in living together, and that people who had casually dropped into any inn would have more connection with each other than they, the Oblonsky family and household.**

**Oblonsky's wife refused to leave her room; he himself hadn't been home for three days. The children were running around the house as though lost; the English governess had had a quarrel with the housekeeper and written to a friend of hers asking her to look out for a new job for her; the day before the cook had picked**

**dinnertime to go out; the kitchenmaid and coachman had given notice.**

Here we have the bold, memorable (and famous) opening sentence, followed by a quick summary of all that has happened recently. Once we've been brought up to date, by this efficient method, then the real book begins. This kind of opening is more like a prologue.

Not just in the opening, but through a book 'show don't tell' is a useful motto. Perhaps it can be taken too far though, as the passage from Thomas Hardy's *Tess of the d'Urbevilles* quoted in 'Euphemisms' shows (page 27).

## SUMMARY

♦ Be stingy.

♦ Be cool.

♦ Understate.

♦ Plain English is usually best.

♦ Monitor your use of adverbs.

♦ Show, don't tell.

# Banality

There's a joke about two people who are having a competition in banality. They go into a famous art gallery. 'My, look at that painting,' says one of them, 'that's a big one.' 'Yes,' says the other, 'and it's shiny too.'

Good gag, hey? Well, once you've dried your eyes and regained control of your bladder we'll press on. The message is that banality is boring. Knowing what to leave out of a story is often as important as knowing what to put in. Leave out the banal details. No one wants a long description of what was eaten for breakfast, unless it's got special significance. If a vegetarian has lamb's fry, that's interesting. Or if a person who is unhappy won't eat breakfast. Or an argument breaks out during the toast and coffee.

One would think that characters in books shouldn't be too banal, though again there are daring exceptions to this rule. Look at the celebrated short story 'The Secret Life of Walter Mitty', by James Thurber. Mitty is one of the most banal characters ever to appear in fiction, but we soon realise that he escapes from his humdrum life by daydreaming. Even his daydreams are banal but Thurber's story succeeds because we wryly realise that Mitty is everyman; we recognise ourselves in him.

Judith Hearne, in Brian Moore's book *The Lonely Passion of Judith Hearne*, appears to live a banal life but we become engrossed in her pitiful day-by-day struggles to exist, especially in her attempts to improve her condition.

More frequently a writer will endow characters with some special characteristic that makes them obviously interesting. Most of the siblings in J. D. Salinger's *Raise High the Roof-Beam Carpenters* are adults when the book begins, but all share an extraordinary past: they have, in their childhoods, been regular participants in a national radio children's quiz show.

Paul Zindel, author of *The Pigman*, creates a major character called Mr Pignati who makes jokes about his name and collects toy pigs for a hobby. The protagonist in Glenda Adams's *Dancing on Coral* not only has an unusual name (Lark) but has a father who spends the whole book building a box in which he eventually has himself shipped overseas.

As a variation, an author might write about an ordinary person in an extraordinary situation. Anton Steenwijk, in *The Assault* by Dutch writer Harry Mulisch, is rather a dull character, but when he was twelve his family was slain in horrifying circumstances by the Nazis. We become engrossed by Mulisch's account of how Anton's life is shadowed by this event.

Few characters come duller than Pip in Charles Dickens's *Great Expectations* but who cares? He is always at the centre of such a rich collection of events and characters that we hardly notice his banality. Among the people he encounters are Miss Havisham, who was jilted at the altar many years ago and, a mad old woman now, still sits surrounded by the remnants of her wedding feast; Wemmick, who has built himself a little house with a drawbridge and moat; Estella, who has been deliberately raised so that she will not know or understand love: a cold young woman 'programmed' to break men's hearts; and an odd-job man in a riverside pub, who dresses in the clothes of drowned men he pulls from the water.

It is also important to avoid banality in style. I'd call this pop song banal:

You are my special angel, sent from up above,
My fate smiled down on me and sent an angel to love,
You are my special angel, right from paradise,
I know that you're an angel, heaven is in your eyes.

A smile from your lips brings the summer sunshine,
The tears from your eyes bring the rain.
I feel your touch, your warm embrace,
And I'm in heaven again.

You are my special angel through eternity;
I'll have my special angel here to watch over me.

Banal writing like this often relies heavily on cliches, but that's not the full story. It also uses stale images, is shallow, and deals only in the obvious.

At the other end of the spectrum to pop music are hymns, but they can be equally banal:

Every morning the red sun
Rises warm and bright
But the evening cometh on
And the dark, cold night
There's a bright land far away,
Where 'tis never-ending day.

Every spring the sweet young flowers
Open bright and gay,
Till the chilly autumn hours
Wither them away.
There's a land we have not seen
Where the trees are always green.

It's often true of banal writing that it doesn't resemble real life, just a superficial, idealised world. Look at the first four lines of the hymn for example. Is the sun always red at dawn? Is every night dark and cold?

It was a bright, beautiful, warm day when our ship spread her canvas to the breeze, and sailed for the regions of the south. Oh, how my heart bounced with delight as I listened to the merry chorus of the sailors, while they hauled at the ropes and got in the anchor! The captain shouted; the men ran to obey; the noble ship bent over to the breeze, and the shore gradually faded from my view, while I stood looking on with a kind of feeling that the whole was a delightful dream.

This is from R. M. Ballantyne's *The Coral Island*. The narrator, Ralph, soon makes friends with two other boys. Incidentally, note the way Ballantyne seems to use adjectives in groups of three:

There were a number of boys on the ship, but two of them were my special favourites. Jack Martin was a tall, strapping, broadshouldered youth of eighteen, with a handsome good-humoured, firm face. He had had a good education, was clever and hearty and lion-like in his actions, but mild and quiet in disposition. Jack was a general favourite, and had a particular fondness for me. My other companion was Peterkin Gay. He was little, quick, funny, decidedly mischievous, and about fourteen years old. But Peterkin's mischief was almost always harmless, else he could not have been so much beloved as he was.

'Hello, youngster!' cried Jack Martin, giving me a slap on the shoulder, the day I joined the ship. 'Come below, and I'll show you your berth. You and I are to be messmates, and I think we shall be good friends, for I like the look o' you!'

Jack was right. He and I and Peterkin afterwards became the best and staunchest friends that ever tossed together on the stormy waves.

Well, we'll have to leave Ralph and Peterkin Gay tossing together on the stormy waves and move on. Here's some more sophisticated banality from Wibur Smith's *Golden Fox*:

Then abruptly her pulse checked and then raced away again. In her ears the music took on a sweeter, more cheerful note, the oppressive crowds and the noise seemed to recede, her dark mood evaporated miraculously, and she was borne up on a wave of excitement and wild anticipation.

There he was, standing in the front doorway. He was so tall that he towered half a head above those around him. A single lock of hair had fallen like a question mark on to his forehead, and his expression was remote, almost contemptuous.

She wanted to shout his name. 'Ramon, here I am!' But she restrained herself, and set aside her glass without looking. It toppled over and the girl on the step below her exclaimed as lukewarm champagne cascaded down her bare back. Isabella did not even hear her protest. She came to her feet in one fluid movement, and instantly, Ramon's cool green gaze was on her.

They looked at each other over the heads of the swirling, gyrating dancers and it was as though the two of them were completely alone. Neither of them smiled. It seemed to Isabella that this was a solemn moment. He had come, and in some vague way she sensed the significance of what was happening. She was certain that in that instant her life had changed. Nothing would ever be the same again.

She began to descend, and she did not stumble over the sprawling, embracing couples that clogged the staircase. They seemed to open before her, and her feet found their own way between them.

She was watching Ramon. He had not moved to meet her. He stood very still in the giddy throng. His stillness reminded her of one of the great predatory African cats, and she felt a tiny thrill of fear, an exhilaration of the blood as she went down to him.

When she stood before him, neither of them spoke, and after a moment she lifted her tanned bare arms towards him and as he took her to his chest she wound her arms around his neck. They danced and she found

**every movement of his body transmitted to her own like a current of electricity.**

**The music was superfluous; they moved to a rhythm of their own.**

Even the first sentence of this extract is flawed, with its repetition of 'then'.

It's strange that so many writers of thrillers aren't able to write about women convincingly. Their female characters seem two-dimensional, and their love scenes stilted and incredible. The image of two lovers whose eyes meet across a crowded room at a party is so banal that it would take a great stylist to make it work. Unfortunately Smith's no stylist. Tired vague statements like '... her life had changed. Nothing would ever be the same again' are just 'fillers', which avoid a realistic exploration of the character's feelings. The sexist image of the remote contemptuous male standing aloof in the distance, while the woman crawls over broken glass (almost literally) to get to him is a common male fantasy but has nothing to do with real life relationships. Hackneyed metaphors ('she was borne up on a wave of excitement'), ridiculous images ('her feet found their own way between them'), and cliches ('they moved to a rhythm of their own') make *Golden Fox* about as worthwhile as a telephone directory. You can write better than this.

Oh, by the way: Wilbur Smith has been the world's biggest-selling English-language author for the last quarter of the twentieth century. Now how do you explain that?

# Language of Banality

In 1946 an Australian scientist, Eric Ashby, wrote in 'Challenge to Education' that 'the child becomes convinced that the seven deadly sins at school are: originality, resource, scepticism, critical judgement, non-conformity, lack of deference to those in authority, and wanting to know more than is in the syllabus'. Nothing much has changed. In the area of language, in particular, children are programmed from birth, like computers, to use language in certain patterns. Hence when we hear the word 'ocean' we feel almost compelled to call it sparkling and blue. Birds always twitter, leaves rustle and lightning flashes. Babies are little and cute, people over sixty are old and wrinkled and wise (one thing I liked about *The Secret Diary of Adrian Mole* was that Bert Baxter, the old-age pensioner, drank, smoke, smelt and didn't pay his bills). The sun sets, night falls, darkness descends, the moon rises, stars come out (twinkling or sparkling or both), wolves howl, birds fly overhead (as distinct from underfoot), somewhere in the distance . . .

Sound familiar? Once you've mastered these patterns you can churn out airport novels at a rate of a quarter of a million words a year as quite a few people do. You don't have to think when you write like this; the computer in your head does the work for you. You can have the television on or listen to your Walkman as you write.

It's not very satisfying though. For one thing it's not an expression of your personality. It doesn't have your individual stamp on it, and the best writing always has that.

Lots of phrases come straight from the data bank of cliches. When you come across this kind of writing: 'It cannot be doubted that . . .', 'this great country of ours . . .', 'achieving excellence', 'maximising the potential of every individual', you know that a human being wrote it, but he or she got lost inside there somewhere.

Have a look at any school's statement of its goals. There's a good chance you'll find this kind of language.

The process works like this: suppose you're writing about honey, and you want an adjective to go with that noun. The computer-in-your-head obligingly flashes up a word: 'sweet'. That's the end of the operation for the bad writer – he or she uses 'sweet' with no further thought. The good writer though, disappointed with 'sweet', presses the reject button.

Immediately the computer provides another word (it's a very efficient computer): 'golden'.

Again the good writer, searching for something less banal, rejects it. So it goes on: 'sticky', 'fresh', 'delicious'. Eventually you come to a barrier. It seems like the end:

**sweet**
**golden**
**sticky**
**fresh**
**delicious**

For the good writer, this is not an end, it's a beginning. It's only now that real writing takes place. The good writer reaches through the barrier, into the vast open space where anything can happen. New adjectives can be generated; at last there's some original thought and language usage. Molten honey perhaps. Runny honey. Trickling honey. Creeping, slithering, sliding honey.

This kind of writing is more difficult because it takes thought and concentration. You might have to turn off the television or put down the Walkman. But the more you do it, the more natural and simple it becomes.

Be warned though: most pieces of writing can only sustain a few examples of really original language. It can become artificial, cloying, off-putting if overdone. It depends on your style of course. Here's D. H. Lawrence in *Kangaroo* describing the Australian bush:

**Even the few birds seemed to be swamped in silence.**
**Waiting, waiting – the bush seemed to be hoarily waiting.**
**And he could not penetrate its secret. He couldn't get at**
**it. Nobody could get at it. What was it waiting for?**
**And then one night at the time of the full moon he**
**walked alone into the bush. A huge electric moon, huge,**
**and the tree trunks like naked pale Aborigines among the**

**dark-soaked foliage, in the moonlight. And not a sign of**
**life, not a vestige ...**

This poem is called 'One Summer'. It's by Steve Turner:

**One summer you**
**aeroplaned away**
**too much money**
**away for me, and**
**stayed there for**
**quite a few**
**missed entrances.**
**Before leaving,**
**you smiled me that**
**you'd return all of**
**a mystery moment and**
**would airletter me**
**every few breakfasts**
**in the meantime.**
              **This**
**you did, and I thank**
**you most kissingly.**
                   **I**
**wish however, that I**
**could hijackerplane**
**to the Ignited States**
**of Neon where I'd**
**crash land perfectly**
**in the deserted**
**airport of your heart.**

You might like to go through these two pieces, by Lawrence
and Turner, and highlight the moments when they've used
language in a fresh and unusual way. Then ask yourself:
Have they got the balance about right? Have they overdone
it? Or is their writing predictable and programmed?

    Perhaps the most obvious area where language too easily

gets stuck in a rut is the area of simile and metaphor. 'Stuck in a rut' is a good example; what an overworked phrase it is! Try this test: unscramble the words below. As soon as you work out what each one is, write the word that immediately occurs to you as a comparison. So if you start with RKAD, decode it as DARK and write the first word that leaps into your head to complete the phrase 'as dark as'. No cheating though! It has to be the very first word!

**TWEIH**
**WLOS**
**HTLIG**
**ADDE**

Do a quick survey. For the first one how many people wrote 'snow' or 'ghost'? For 'slow', 'snail'? Or 'wet week' or 'turtle' or 'tortoise'? For 'light', 'feather'? For 'dead', 'doornail', or 'dodo'? You see how well everyone has been programmed to always connect certain words. It's a big challenge for a writer to break that programming.

A reminder though: good simple straightforward writing is often the best style, especially if you've got a strong story to tell. But you should still avoid cliches, or phrases like 'at death's door', 'knew full well', 'made a promising start', 'blown to smithereens', 'truth is stranger than fiction' and 'got up on the wrong side of the bed'.

Try some new comparisons for the following list.

**as slow as**
**as heavy as**
**as dead as**
**as fast as**
**as red as**
**as happy as**

Often comparisons with abstractions work well: as light as love, as dark as death, as deep as time.

Another exercise in making new connections works like

this: list half-a-dozen nouns down one side of a page and half-a-dozen adjectives or verbs down the other. Then connect them at random.

| ADJECTIVES | NOUNS |
|---|---|
| green | grass |
| bubbly | champagne |
| bony | skeleton |
| squawking | parrot |
| striped | zebra |
| electronic | watch |
| exploding | bomb |

Matched in these conventional pairs, these are unexceptional, but when you shuffle a few around you suddenly enter a world of new images. An exploding watch? Striped grass? Green champagne? Electronic is interesting with just about anything except watch. Some don't work – green parrot, for example, hardly opens up dazzling possibilities.

The interesting thing is that by playing these games with language we're giving ourselves the potential to do something more; we're actually creating new images and thereby new stories, perhaps even new realities. By pairing the words we almost bring these things into existence. 'In the beginning was the word ...' Electronic grass, for instance. You could write a story about that. What does it do, massage your feet as you walk on it? Operate burglar alarms in maximum security institutions? Is it eaten by electronic sheep? What would happen to you if you ran the lawn-mower over it one day?

## SUMMARY

♦ You can describe banal characters or situations if you

do it with style; or if there are other extraordinary elements in the story.

♦ Be adventurous with language.

# Make Something Happen

The great British theatre director Peter Brook has been quoted as advising his actors, when they 'freeze' during improvisation games: 'Keep going! Make something happen!'

This is good advice for writing too. When you feel the story start to drag – and most do at some stage or other – then it's time to 'make something happen'. Kill someone. Have someone win a prize. Have a giant hand come up through the floor, grab a character by the ankles and drag her or him away. Have two people fall in love. Have three people fall in love. Have an orgy. You're God when you're writing; you can do anything. The only unforgivable sin is to be boring.

Here's a good exercise. Separate into pairs and designate yourself A and B, or Q and E if you're sick of A and B. Decide who's going to start. Right, that's the hard part out of the way. Now supposing it's B who starts. B begins telling a story to A. Any old story, the more boring the better. As soon as A notices that the story is taking a boring or predictable path, she or he contradicts with 'No, you didn't', and B is forced onto a new track.

For example:

**B: I woke up this morning, got up and got dressed ...**
**A: No you didn't.**
**B: Oh OK, I didn't. I stayed in bed and went back to sleep.**
**A: (*Still bored*) No you didn't.**
**B: Oh. Well, I crawled under the bed, where I found my baby brother, who we'd been looking for since the weekend (*this is better*). He was quite hungry, so I gave him a biscuit.**

A: No you didn't.
B: No, I ordered a pizza, which arrived half an hour later. The pizza was really good ...
A: No it wasn't.
B: No, in fact it was so rubbery we used it for a frisbee.

Now this isn't going to sell a million, but that's not the point. After doing the exercise a few times you should try to apply it to written work. But now, instead of your partner's voice ringing in your ears (another cliche) you have to reproduce his or her voice inside your head. When you find your story becoming too stale, too routine, hear that voice calling:

'Jump!' the sergeant shouted. With my heart in my mouth I jumped. ['Oh help,' sighs the teacher. 'Please let it not be another war story. And "heart in my mouth" is such a cliche.'] Luckily the parachute opened, and I found myself floating gently to earth. I landed on the hard sand. [NO! NO! No, you didn't.] I landed in the world's biggest passionfruit sponge cake? I landed back in the plane after an updraught caught me? I landed in the twenty-third century? [No, we're going to be realistic.] To my horror I landed in the middle of two rows of tents. A sentry saw me and shouted, then began firing. I pressed the release button on the parachute which blew towards him and blocked his view. I ran in the opposite direction. [No, you didn't.] OK, strike that. I ran to a parked vehicle. [No, too easy.] I ducked into a tent that looked empty. [No, it wasn't.] There were two men asleep in sleeping bags. I backed out. [No, you didn't.] I crawled into the nearest sleeping bag and pretended to be asleep ...

It's not to everyone's taste, but it's got a bit of tension. Of course you can go too far and put your protagonist in an impossible situation. But the makers of the film *Butch*

*Cassidy and the Sundance Kid* even found a way out of that for their two stars. Well, sort of.

Movies are a good illustration of this 'No, you didn't' exercise. Take car chases for example. Among the early movie car chases were those in *The Italian Job, Bullit* and *The French Connection*. They were wildly exciting to us unsophisticated children of the sixties. As time went on, though, every movie, even every hour-long police drama on television, had its obligatory car chase. One of the sights of those days was to watch *Homicide* and see Melbourne detectives trying to do in a Falcon what American cops were doing with Harley Davidsons and Mustangs.

When the car chases inevitably became stale, no longer holding viewers' attention, writers of action movies had to press their 'No, you didn't' buttons. The cop, on a Harley, chases the crook in a Cadillac? No he doesn't, it's been done too often. OK, so the hero in a speedboat chases the crooks in another speedboat across land and water (a James Bond). Or, the cops in hundreds of police cars chase the good guys in their beat-up old wreck (*The Blues Brothers*). Or, the getaway car splits in half, completely confusing the pursuers (*Malcolm*).

You can see that creative people are never content to copy someone else's ideas. They copy, yes, but they improve too. So, we have plane chases, train, horse, spaceship, helicopter, bulldozer chases. *The Back to the Future* movies pioneered the skateboard chase. I remember James Bond being chased in a double-decker bus, and going under a low bridge with spectacular results.

# Status

Many societies of living creatures, including humans, have a kind of status hierarchy. In Australia, presumably the Governor-General and the Prime Minister would be near the top, but everyone's perspective is different; a great artist or sportsplayer or singer or actor might have higher status than the Prime Minister, for some people.

What's the status hierarchy in your city or district?

Most schools have well-established hierarchies. The usual structure has a principal at the top, then senior teachers, then other teachers, then prefects and/or senior students, and so on down to the youngest students. This model ignores a lot of people and situations though; where would you place the maintenance staff and cleaners for example? The secretarial staff? Can a Year 10 student ever have more status than a Year 12? What happens if a teacher has less status or power than some of the students? If you want to read about a school that has no hierarchy, track down a book called *Summerhill* by A. S. Neill.

How does your school help bolster the status of its teachers? In many classrooms the teachers have a raised platform at the front. Is it so the students can see the teachers better, or is it to do with status?

You could spend a lifetime studying the subtleties of status and still be learning at the end of that lifetime. It's an important topic though, because status permeates every aspect of our lives – families, for example.

In writing, it is often changes in status which give a story tension, comedy or tragedy. Consider this scene:

Rob knocked on the door.

'Come in,' the principal said.

Rob entered the room and said, 'I've been sent to you for smoking.'

'Yes, I know,' the principal said. 'And it's not good enough. This is the third time in a fortnight.'

Pretty weak scene, huh? Try it again, adding the details that will show the status of the two people.

Rob tapped nervously on the door.

'Enter,' the principal shouted.

Rob slipped into the room and stood just inside the door. The principal was busy writing and did not look up. But as she wrote she suddenly said: 'Closer.'

Rob moved three short steps nearer to the desk. Finally Ms Rhodes stopped writing, put down the pen and leaned forward, looking hard at Rob. Rob peered at his feet, studying the size of his shoes.

'Robert Chance,' she said, in a loud slow voice.

'Yea, Miss,' Rob whispered, hoping she couldn't smell the tobacco.

If by some freak of education you didn't know what a principal was, you could still work out the status of the two players in this scene. With those details in the scene, it is brought to life, made realistic and given tension.

Let's play with the scene a little longer, repeating it with one change. That change, the only change, will be to swap the status of the two people:

Rob threw open the door and strode into the room.

'This is the limit,' he said. 'Three times in two weeks you've taken me away from my Physics class. You'd better have a good reason.'

He spoke softly but every word could be heard. Ms Rhodes jumped up.

'Oh Rob,' she said, 'I'm awfully sorry. Please sit

down ... no, have my chair, it's more comfortable. I do
apologise ... it's just ... the teachers have been
complaining again ...'

'So?'

'Well, it's just ... your smoking ... you see, I am the
principal ...'

'So?'

'Oh nothing ... I just thought ... '

Rob shook out a cigarette from a half crushed packet
in his shirt pocket. Ms Rhodes hurriedly lit it for him,
with a hand that trembled.

Don't you wish life was like that? Maybe it is in your school?

How many movies can you name in which comedy is created
by a change of status – *Annie? Kindergarten Cop? Beverley Hills
Cop?* The famous 'call that a knife' scene in *Crocodile Dundee?*
Bottom's role in *A Midsummer Night's Dream?*

The same is true in romance, too: *Cinderella, Pretty in Pink,
Pretty Woman.* In each film the difference in status between
the lovers provides most of the interest. The audience is
agog: can the gap be bridged? (It says something about our
society that it's nearly always a low status woman and a high
status man.)

Think about all the cops-and-robbers and Western movies
you've seen, too – they are status battles.

And in tragedy. *King Lear* is the story of a great and powerful king with three daughters. As he's growing old he
decides to divide his kingdom between them, and spend the
rest of his life living in comfort with each of them in turn.
One of them isn't obsequious enough to get her share but
the other two are keen, and crawl enough to get half each.
The trouble is, once they get their hands on everything their
father has, they lose interest in him. He is reduced to
poverty, and wanders through the countryside, lost and
lonely, his mind and body both giving way under the strain
of their betrayal.

The play is a tragedy of epic and powerful dimensions. And one element in the tragedy is King Lear's loss of status, from king to poor lost soul. His loss of status is made more poignant by the fact that it was his own vanity and lack of judgement, and betrayal by his own children, that brought it about.

Elements of status are present in nearly all fiction writing. American writer Norman Mailer has been quoted as saying that writers need a 'huge interest' in power; it's a theme that they should be constantly exploring. He claims that if you don't have that interest you'll write 'anaemic' stories. Status and power are closely related. In our society status is influenced by things like occupation, possessions, race, age, accent, personality. It has been influenced by gender, too. Is it still, do you think? What else influences status? Try writing an analysis of a novel or film in which you consider how changes in status have contributed to its effect.

Exploring status through drama and roleplay is a good way of understanding its subtleties better. Try some of these scenes:

Changes of status scenes like the one in the principal's office. Always play them 'straight' first, then repeat with the status changed. For example: a scene in an exclusive restaurant where the customers are rude and demanding and the waiter obsequious – then the opposite.

A conversation in which three or four people try to go slightly higher than each other in status with each comment. The increment has to be slight and the conversation has to be believable. Or try going slightly lower each time (find the famous Monty Python 'We were so poor that . . .' scene, where the actors appear to be going lower but are in fact going higher).

A scene where new people join the group all the time and

each new person has a higher status than the ones before.

A scene where a person thinks he/she has high status, but the others know she/he doesn't.

A monologue by someone who had high status but has lost it.

Body language is an important indicator of status. Think back to the scene with the principal. The way she does not look up when Rob enters the room ... the way she leans forward across the desk ... the way Rob knocks on the door ... all these details of body language help make the scene authentic, because they show us (without telling us) what the principal's status is vis-a-vis Rob.

What other aspects of body language can be used this way? How do high status people sit? Stand? Walk? Where do they sit? How do they use their hands? The jabbing finger, for example, is an indication of very high status.

## SUMMARY

♦ Know the status of the characters in your story.
♦ Include details that will help show their status.
♦ Use changes of status to give the story tension.

# Detail, Detail, Detail

One of the things that separates good writers from the rest is that the rest don't use detail when they write. Or if they do, they don't use it well. We looked at detail a little when discussing status in the last section, but let's look at it more closely now.

I hope when you were younger your father or mother did you a favour by playing family games like 'I spy'. These games are valuable because they teach you to be observant, and few attributes matter more to the writer. Here's an exercise you can do with a group of people that'll give an idea of how difficult it is to be observant.

Pick a common object: one key on a key ring, for example. With the group sitting in a circle pass the object around. Each person has to name one characteristic of it that no one else has mentioned already. By the time the object has gone around a few times, so that sixty or eighty characteristics of it have been named, the exercise starts to get quite difficult. Keep going! (A hint: remember to use all the senses.)

## Detail in Character

'Worship the divine detail', said famous writer Vladimir Nabokov.

There are at least three times in every piece of writing when you should use detail.

The first is when you're describing an important character. If the character is central to the story it's not enough to say that he or she is '1.7m tall with black hair'. Half the population fits that description. There are earlier examples in this book where writers made characters more distinctive by identifying special characteristics. To make your major characters come to life you must endow them with unique details. Something about the way they dress, for example? The jewellery they wear? Do they have tattoos, braces, glasses, facial hair, make-up, painted nails? Is there something odd about them? Perhaps they wear two watches, or carry a spare pair of socks in their pocket, or wear a badge with a picture of Big Bird.

Of course it's in their attitudes, opinions, thoughts, personalities that your characters will truly express their uniqueness, but the little details of dress and appearance help.

Think about behaviour too. Perhaps you could have a character chewing the back of their hand whenever they listen to someone, or refusing to speak when they drive, or irritatingly humming the same tune for weeks on end. These mannerisms are all important to help the reader think of people as individuals.

# Detail in Setting

The second area where detail is needed is in descriptions of significant places. Those settings have to be brought to life, be they houses, towns, cities, nations or anywhere else. Again it helps if you bring your powers of observation to bear. Start with your own flat, house or caravan. We know it's got a roof, walls and a floor, a door and window. Or we hope it does. But what can you find that gives it its special atmosphere? How can you describe its unique flavour? Here's an example from *David Copperfield* by Charles Dickens:

**I gazed upon the schoolroom into which he took me, as the most forlorn and desolate place I had ever seen. I see it now. A long room, with hats and slates. Scraps of old copy-boards, and exercises litter the desks. Two miserable little white mice, left behind by their owner, are running**

up and down in a fussy castle made of pasteboard and wire, looking in all the corners with their red eyes for anything to eat. A bird, in a cage very little bigger than himself, makes a mournful rattle now and then in hopping on his perch, two inches high, or dropping from it; but neither sings nor chirps. There is a strange unwholesome smell upon the room, like mildewed corduroys, sweet apples wanting air, and rotten books. There could not well be more ink splashed about it, if it had been roofless from its first construction, and the skies had rained, snowed, hailed and blown ink through the various seasons of the year.

## Detail for Tension

The third situation where detail is usually especially effective is demonstrated in the following piece of writing from Harper Lee's *To Kill a Mockingbird*. The scene is a court-room; the lawyer, Atticus, is about to ask the witness, Mr Ewell, a question. As you read the extract, note the extraordinary detail provided ... all of it leading to the question itself, which in a different context would seem innocuous. What's the effect of all this detail? What is it signalling to the reader? What does it tell us about the request which comes at the end?

Atticus was reaching into the inside pocket of his coat. He drew out an envelope, then reached into his vest pocket and unclipped his fountain pen. He moved leisurely, and had turned so that he was in full view of the jury. He unscrewed the fountain pen cap and placed it gently on his table. He shook the pen a little, then handed it with the envelope to the witness. 'Would you write your name for us?' he asked. 'Clearly now, so the jury can see you do it.'

Lee is demonstrating the power of detail in creating a sense of tension. Here, the detail signals that 'Would you write your name for us?' is vital. So, the third area where detail is useful is in signalling an important moment, a climax. If I write: 'I walked to the door, opened it, and went inside', then what have I got? Not much. But how about this:

**I walked towards the old green door. It hadn't been painted for a long time: the paint was peeling and cracking. I put my hand on the rusty door knob, turned it a few centimetres to the right, and pushed. The door scraped open, leaving a long white scratch on the wooden floor. I took one step, into the room.**

Now I have indicated to the reader that something very important is going to happen inside that room.

If you still think detail isn't important, let's finish with these two extracts from recent newspaper film reviews:

**In cameraman Franz Planer's black and white photography . . . almost every shot is memorable. They capture the poetry of the small gesture: a tilt of the head, a breath of wind catching a lock of hair and tiny, but expressive movements of the camera in which one elegant composition glides into another. Long afterwards, these images haunt you.**

And for contrast:

**. . . writer-director Chris Columbus assumes . . . that his audience are fools who will overlook the film's lack of attention to detail.**

As in film, so in writing. Don't assume that your readers are fools who will overlook your lack of attention to detail.

## SUMMARY

♦ Use detail for significant people and places in a story.
♦ Use detail to create tension.

# Names

Funnily enough, choosing names is one of the things I find hardest about writing. Among the reference books beside me when I write are a dictionary of surnames, a dictionary of first names, some old class rolls, a telephone directory, a postcode book, and a dictionary of mythology. I dip into them all the time for names of people and places, but even with their help it can take hours to get the right ones.

Names are important though. Sometimes even the sound of the name can suggest what kind of person a character is. Take Mr Jaggers in Charles Dickens's *Great Expectations.* What kind of profession might he follow? What's his personality likely to be? Or Mr Pumblechook, in the same book – would you want him as a friend? How about Mr Squeers in *Nicholas Nickleby,* also by Dickens.

Tolkien had the same kind of feeling for names. Of the following characters from *Lord of the Rings,* which ones do you think might be good and which ones evil? What do you sense about them from their names?

**Gollum, Strider, Mr Butterbur**
**Gandalf, Fangorn, Grimbold**
**Pippin, Wormtongue, Shagrat**
**Mordor, Merry, Thorin Oakenshield**

Here's a selection of names from an old English school story called *Fifth Form at St Dominic's* by Talbot Baines Reed:

**Loman, Ricketts, Padger**
**Cripps, Dr Senior, Bullinger**
**Bramble, Greenfield**

There are obviously at least two good guys and two bad here, though Bramble and Padger are neither good nor bad, just messy ink-stained juniors who are like rowdy animals. In books for young children names are often less subtle; chosen because they sound funny or give obvious indications about the people to whom they refer. In Mary Steele's books, for example, we have characters such as Mr Wanderlust, Mrs Woollybutt and Captain Chilblain.

Names can be chosen for a deeper significance. In the Bible are two famous brothers, Cain and Abel, sons of Adam and Eve. In jealous rage, Cain kills Abel. Their names (sometimes with different spelling) are often used by writers nowadays for characters who were, or should have been, as close as brothers, but have had a 'falling out'. There's *The Caine Mutiny* by Herman Wouk, where navy officers in wartime, who need to work closely together, mutiny and take over the ship, and eventually start fighting among themselves. In *Citizen Kane*, the Orson Welles movie, we see a man who betrays his two wives and his friends. There's even a 1936 movie romance called *Cain and Mabel* and a Jeffrey Archer novel, *Kane and Abel*.

Stephen Spielberg's first big success was *Duel*, the classic road film of a battle between a semitrailer and a car. If you watch the film closely you can see how Spielberg intended it to work on several levels: the car driver represents Mr Average, the ordinary, soft, modern man, who in the movie is catapulted back to the Stone Age where he has to rediscover cunning and toughness before he can defeat the 'dragon' (the truck). Spielberg gives this everyday person a perfect name: David Mann. David, for the little man who beats the giant, and Mann for the common man whom he represents. But wait! There's more! 'Dave Mann' sounds very much like caveman, doesn't it? And Dave at the end of the film has certainly reverted to caveman status: in the last shot we see him leaping around on top of a cliff, grunting and flapping his arms in triumph.

Australian Murray Bail wrote a book called *Holden's Performance*. He has been quoted as saying that he chose the name Holden for the main character because Holden is always on the move. In the book Holden goes to the Sydney beachside suburb of Manly, because Holden is becoming more masculine.

In the movie *It's a Wonderful Life* the villain is Mr Potter, who wants to develop a housing estate called 'Potter's Field'. Observant viewers would remember that in the Bible Potters Field was the place bought with the money paid to Judas for betraying Jesus. Graham Greene's novel *A Burnt Out Case* is about an architect called Querry – a name chosen to reflect the man's quest for meaning in his life. Nurse Ratchett in Ken Kesey's *One Flew Over the Cuckoo's Nest* continually tightens her grip on the ward, forcing everybody in the direction she wants them to go, just like a real ratchet. Mandy, in my book *Letters from the Inside*, is sometimes referred to by the nickname 'Manna'. Manna is a kind of spiritual food, a gift from Heaven, and that is the role Mandy plays in the life of her friend Tracey.

# The Senses

Some blind people can walk into a room and tell you who's been there simply by using their sense of smell. It's said that Koori people could track a person through the bush by their smell. In France children were often used instead of pigs to sniff out truffles, a delicacy growing underground. (Children were preferred to adults because their sense of smell is stronger.)

We all have remarkable sensory powers but as the world becomes more automated we use them less and less and so they atrophy. If you want to see how powerful they could become, look at someone who's lost one or more of their senses. Blind people often develop remarkable hearing. Hence the autobiography of Tom Sullivan, a blind American, is called *If You Could See What I Hear*. Deaf people often have sharp eyesight, notice tiny details, and have particularly good peripheral vision.

Helen Keller was blind and deaf. In her autobiography *The Story of My Life* she describes a thunderstorm. She is sitting in a tree:

**Suddenly a change passed over the tree. All the sun's warmth left the air. I knew the sky was black, because all the heat, which meant light to me, had died out of the atmosphere. A strange odour came up from the earth. I knew it, it was the odour that always precedes a thunderstorm, and a nameless fear clutched at my heart. I felt absolutely alone, cut off from my friends and the firm earth. The immense, the unknown, enfolded me. I remained still and expectant; a chilling terror crept over**

me. I longed for my teacher's return; but above all things I wanted to get down from that tree.

There was a moment of sinister silence, then a multitudinous stirring of the leaves. A shiver ran through the tree, and the wind sent forth a blast that would have knocked me off had I not clung to the branch with might and main. The tree swayed and strained. The small twigs snapped and fell about me in showers. A wild impulse to jump seized me, but terror held me fast. I crouched down in the fork of the tree. The branches lashed about me. I felt an intermittent jarring, that came now and then, as if something heavy had fallen and the shock had travelled up till it reached the limb I sat on.

No human being, as far as I know, has challenged herself or himself to develop the five senses to their maximum. It would be a fascinating thing to do, for their potential may be unlimited. Imagine having the eyes of an eagle (who can see movement three kilometres away), the ears of a dog, the nose of a rat. You'd be a pretty funny looking person. I don't know which creature has the most sensitive skin or taste buds – perhaps it's the human being. Certainly wine connoisseurs, after years of training and practice, can identify not just the country the grapes were grown in, but the district, the vineyard, and the year that the wine was produced.

As the world moves towards greater homogeneity we risk losing these powers. Instead of valuing variety and appreciating how interesting subtle differences are, companies like McDonald's make it their business to produce billions of hamburgers throughout the world, each one absolutely identical. Fruit and vegetable producers have followed the same path, sacrificing variety of shape, texture, aroma and taste for products which are all the same shape (so they pack better) and which last longer. But this is not just true of food; it happens with buildings, cars, clothes, language. We need to learn to value diversity once more.

A writer must develop his/her senses as much as possible and use them actively when writing. A description of a storm that doesn't include its smell will not convince a reader. A description of a flower will often be enhanced by including the feel of the petals, leaves and stalks. It's astonishing how many people try to write about food without mentioning its smell. But here's an extract from Kampoon Boontawee's novel *A Child of the North-East*.

**The two kratongs were filled with the (ant) eggs and the queen ants. Koon's mother sprinkled them with salt and Kamgong carefully poured water over them until it nearly reached the top. Then they placed them over the fire, and soon tiny bubbles began to rise. For a brief moment, the queen ants, which had been floating about, beat their wings rapidly, then were still. Roon's mother spooned a bit of pla ra into each kratong, turned to Uncle Gah and said, 'You taste it for us.'**

**'Nobody has to taste it,' he replied. 'The smell went up my nose, and my mouth is full of saliva already.'**

**Koon thought that Uncle Gah was right. The smell was enough to tell anyone how good it would taste. He went to his cart for rice boxes, and as he walked back toward the fire his mother called out, 'Everyone come now. The gaeng is done.'**

**When they had formed their circle, Uncle Kem looked around and asked, 'Why hasn't anyone brought fish or roasted frogs?'**

**Everyone laughed, and Uncle Gah said, 'You go to your cart and get fish and frogs, and you eat them. I am eating only this gaeng.'**

**'These spoons are too short,' Jundi complained, frowning into a kratong at the mass of eggs that lay in the bottom. 'I can't even get any of the eggs, only juice.'**

'You are supposed to sip the fragrant juices first,' Uncle Gah said. 'And dip your rice into jaew. Then, when all the juices are gone, and you are not so hungry, you eat the eggs.'

In our society we have become heavily reliant on sight, perhaps too much so. To describe the way something looks is not the only way to evoke a scene. Here's how Dickens uses smell in *Bleak House*:

**It is somewhere about five or six o'clock in the afternoon, and a balmy fragrance of warm tea hovers in Cook's court. It hovers about Sangsby's door.**

In *How Green Was My Valley*, by Richard Llewellyn, this wonderful description of a boy trying to get out from his upstairs bedroom at night, without his parents knowing, relies mainly on sounds for its effect:

**I was not exactly afraid now that the time had come but my heart was beating so loud I was sure they would hear downstairs. It is strange how loud little sounds become when you are in the dark and doing something wrong.**

**When I got up the old bed creaked so much I could have given it a brick for its trouble, but at last, inch by inch, I was out of it, and even then the bedclothes breathed so loud it was like putting back some old man.**

**The floor, then.**

**Each plank had something to say, scolding and moaning when I put down a foot and picked it up, and the carpet, too, was stretching and grieving all the way to the chest of drawers by the window.**

**To push up that window was to suffer for years, it seemed to me. I held my breath and pulled all sorts of faces as I raised the little sash, ready at the slightest movement downstairs to leap for the bedclothes. Bit by bit it went up, and the more it went, the colder blew the draught, and the more shivering I got, and what between**

**listening for noise downstairs and squeaks in the window, and sounds of somebody coming outside, I got a sort of squint in my ears ...**

For a book which offers a rich exploration of sight, taste, hearing, touch and smell, try *Celebration of the Senses*, by Australian writer Eric Rolls. Rolls, a farmer-poet, writes honestly and deeply of his own senses and sensory experiences. Here is the last paragraph of his description of killing a pig:

**The flow of blood, the flow of squeals stop together. Pig is meat. The water has reached 62 degrees C. We lower the carcass in, move it about for a couple of minutes, then lift it out on to the scraping table. The hair slips off with the paper-thin top skin and the carcass is firm, smooth, white and rounded. A layer of fat about a centimetre deep underlies the thick skin that bubbled into a crisp, aromatic crust, the crackle, on every slice of roast pork.**

In a postscript Rolls makes the astonishing point that he is the first writer ever to undertake such a piece of writing: a celebration of the senses. The book should be given to all school students, if only because of its wonderful explicit descriptions of the loving sexual relationship between Rolls and his wife Joan.

Read his book, then try writing equally honestly of your sensory experiences if you dare.

## SUMMARY

♦ Don't rely on sight alone. Smell, taste, touch and hearing are at least equally important to a writer.

# Cheating to Get Experience

'Write from your own experience!' English teachers are trained from birth to offer this advice to students. There's a lot of value in it, but for fiction writers it has limits. If you're very keen to write books about drug trafficking or film stars or wars and you haven't been involved in anything on that list, then the best advice is probably 'don't'. But if you're determined, then the question is how to write such stories and make them convincing.

It must be possible. Writers of many adventure books, detective novels and thrillers obviously go outside their experience frequently to produce their work. Yet students who write, say, drug stories set in New York often fail. The stories are unconvincing.

Here are two ways of tackling this problem.

One is to use whatever experience you do have, then transfer it to the situation you want to write about. Suppose you want to tell the story of a daring bank raid. OK, instead of robbing a bank yourself, recall a crime you committed as a child, when you stole something, for example, or cheated at school. Now transfer those feelings to the bank raid. Whatever you felt as you planned your offence, as you carried it through and afterwards, whether you were caught or not, probably won't be far different from the emotions of those bank bandits.

You want to write about divorce, but your parents are living together? Recall a time when one parent was away, for whatever reason, and use events and feelings from that time. Drugs? Use moments from dreams you've had, or from a time when you were ill and feverish.

Milk your experiences as much as you can – there's room

for a lot of good novels there. Chances are, though, that the most successful stories you will write will be the ones closest to home, using aspects of your own past and present.

If you're still determined to seek out exotic plots and situations (despite the fact that to people in other parts of the world your life is exotic and fascinating) then the other way to make it convincing is to do some research. The problem with most New York drug stories is that the research consists of students sitting in front of television watching an overblown fantasy with a name like 'Danger Squad' or 'Undercover Patrol'. These give no insight at all. Try instead reading authentic accounts, by people writing honestly about their experiences. When you've read a lot of them, a reasonably accurate picture should start to form. So, to understand life in prison for example, read *Just Us* by Gabrielle Carey or, for life in a psychiatric hospital, *The Treatment* and *The Cure* by Peter Kocan. If you want to write about war, I'd suggest *A Fortunate Life* (A. B. Facey), or *The Naked Island* (Russell Braddon) as background. To understand people's reactions to death, *Year One* by John Tittensor is an account of the author's first year after his children died in a fire. *To Live Until We Say Goodbye* is Dr Elizabeth Kubler-Ross's discussion of the way four different people approached their own deaths. And *Life After Life* (Raymond Moody) opens up some interesting fresh ideas on death through its interviews with people who were clinically dead for short periods of time before being revived.

All of these books are difficult to read – emotionally difficult that is, because they are authentic. They don't deal in slick, superficial feelings of the kind that soap operas and sitcoms exploit. They deal in the uncomfortable raw feelings of people trying to do the best job they can of living their lives. If you read them, and others like them, your writing will change forever. Your reading and viewing might, too, because melodramas will become less satisfying to you. Their limitations will become irritatingly obvious.

## SUMMARY

♦ Transfer feelings from your own experiences to the situations you want to explore in fiction.

♦ Do some research.

# Obeying the Laws of Reality

This won't be easy, trying to convince you that it's OK to have a talking toaster in a story but it's not OK to cook toast in it. Here's the story, or some extracts from it. It was written by a Year 7 girl:

> I woke up at about five-thirty a.m. I was feeling really sick, so I went in to visit my mum. I went into her bedroom. It was so dark in there. I looked over at the bed. She wasn't there! I was horrified. I decided to go get two Disprins and then go back to bed. I did this, then I don't know how, but I fell asleep.

There's the first problem with this piece of writing. Her mother is missing and she just goes back to bed? How likely is that? This story is not obeying the laws of reality. The story continues:

> I woke up two hours later. By this time it was seven-thirty. I went to school.

Same problem again. Her mother's still missing, but she goes to school. That afternoon she returns from school, gets changed and goes to the kitchen. We get this:

> Then suddenly I heard gun shots from the toaster. I thought it had had a malfunction or something. I started to walk over to it. Then suddenly from inside it I heard: 'Wee!! Yeah! Hah!!' but what surprised me even more was that it was my mother's voice! I looked at the toaster, then I looked at the bread basket. I got two pieces of white bread (I was hungry anyway) and I put them into the toaster.

Now, according to some mysterious law of human nature which I don't pretend to understand, the talking toaster is fine. It's an original, imaginative idea, and it works. But to go ahead and cook toast in it, when it's speaking to you in your mother's voice? That's definitely not OK.

Even when writing fantasy there are certain laws of reality that you must obey. When there's danger, people have to feel fear, for example. When someone's shot half a dozen times they have to die. Even heroes have to get tired.

This is from a story by a Year 8 boy. It's about a female bushranger.

**I followed her outside and saw her get on a horse, the second fastest horse on our farm. I jumped on my horse, the fastest on the farm, and followed her out the gate.**

It's a very convenient coincidence that the bushranger takes the second fastest horse. Already we suspect that this story is going to give credibility a hard work-out. The story continues:

**She at last came to a thicket and camped there. Eventually she fell asleep, so I crept up to her bag and took her gun and our family's money and rode back to the house. I rang up the police and told them what had happened and then I ran to the pool, got out all the contents of the overnight bags and put them all in the dryer. While they were drying I woke up Dad and told him also.**

Now he wakes his father? Only now? What kind of family is this? Not one where the laws of reality apply apparently.

Here's a complete story that I wrote in Grade 5. I was proud of it at the time but now it's quite an embarrassment:

**David Jackson and his friend Peter Young were camping out in the rugged Lakes District country. On the first night in camp, after a tea of grilled chops and potatoes,**

they went to bed early. Several hours later, David woke up to hear stealthy footsteps outside. Quickly he woke Peter up and whispered, 'Be quiet you idiot. There's someone rummaging in the haversack.'

Peter sat up. 'Probably some tramp,' he muttered. 'We'll give him a shock.'

The two boys crept silently from the camp. In the moonlight they could see the back of a man searching through their equipment.

'Now!' Peter yelled, and the two leapt upon the man. They heard him mutter a guttural oath and tear himself free. The two boys set off after him at a run. For about ten minutes they followed him through the thick forest, and then he gave them the slip. After a fruitless search they returned to camp, battered and bruised. Satisfied that nothing was missing, they drifted back to sleep.

After an early breakfast, David and Peter set off. They hoped to reach Longmore that evening, where they would spend the night. Naturally, they were discussing the incident of the previous night. At three o'clock they came to Longmore.

'Well, here we are,' David commented. 'Let's have a rest.'

'Look at that old place,' remarked Peter. 'Let's have tea there.'

'OK,' replied David. They were approaching the house, when David pulled Peter into the grass and hissed, 'There are two men going into that house. One of them is the chap who raided our tent last night.' Ten minutes later they crept to one of the windows and heard the men talking.

'You fool!' the older hissed. 'You mean to say that you let two schoolboys beat you. Unless you are more careful in the diamond robbery tonight, you will have to be killed! We will go now.'

'Jump on them when they come out,' whispered Peter.

**As the men appeared, the two boys launched themselves upon them. One let out a groan and fell, the other went down soon after. It is sufficient to say that the police came down and gave the boys five pounds each.**

This little thriller, soon to be filmed by a major Hollywood studio, can be criticised on a number of counts. The language is banal, the plot is boring, there is no characterisation. There are a few moments that are really puzzling too. Why does David call Peter an idiot? What's Peter done wrong? He gets woken in the middle of the night to be called an idiot. That seems a little unfair. But that's nothing compared to the major credibility flaws in the story. How likely is it that these boys would leap on an adult, then chase him through the forest in the darkness? How likely is it that they would then go back to their tents and go to sleep? And later that they would then attack two men and defeat them, where previously they had failed to beat just one? How likely is it that the boy who wrote this story would publish a book on writing when he was older?

There's a limit to the number of coincidences that you can have in a story. How many do you think are reasonable in a full-length novel? One? Two? Three? Certainly my piece has too many. The boys coincidentally see the man who's been ransacking their packs and then the men are coincidentally discussing their crimes just as the boys arrive at the window. (Why would diamond robbers bother ransacking schoolboys' packs anyway?) And so the story reaches its dismal and anticlimactic ending.

Elsewhere in this book you'll find references to feelings, and the importance of using them in writing. One of the laws of reality is that people have feelings. The boys in my story seem to have no feelings, so one law of reality is breached right there.

The more one looks at the story, the more faults one finds. This kind of critical scrutiny needs to be applied to your own writing. If you don't do it yourself, somebody else will!

## SUMMARY

♦ Obey the laws of reality.
♦ Don't rely too heavily on coincidence.

# Sex and Death

These are big issues, among the biggest in our society. They're important to every human being, and anything that's important to human beings is important to a writer. Norman Lindsay once said that the two things you had to include in a book for children were food and fighting. It would be a little foolhardy to say that you should include sex and death in a book for adults, but not many writers exclude them both.

You need to confront sex and death in your writing, and to deal with them in a meaningful way. Perhaps it would be fair to say that the more you've thought about them in your own life, the more you'll be able to write about them. That doesn't mean you've come to terms with either or both of them: some of the most powerful fiction in our culture has been written by people whose attitudes to sex or death could fairly be called neurotic.

The way you write about these things is of course up to you. It hardly needs to be said that writing about them may cause strong reactions from some people. Their reactions will probably tell you more about those people than it will tell you about anything else. Some people are outraged that anyone could dare to write anything that doesn't reflect their own values. But here are some generalisations that may provoke some thought in you:

Every relationship has a sexual element.

For males in our culture, aggression and sex are inextricably linked.

Fear of sex is rampant in Western society.

Humans are the only species who know that they are going to die.

People's fear of death causes them to find all kinds of ways to perpetuate themselves.

Death gives life its point.

Sex and death have a lot in common.

Just grappling with provocative concepts like these can help you write with more insight.

Because these are such powerful subjects it's even more important to write about them with restraint. The strongest horse needs the tightest rein. Charles Dickens was able to wallow in sentimentality when he described the death of Little Nell in *The Old Curiosity Shop*, but those were different times. Fashions change in literature, as in all things. The mood now is for writing that's done with a light touch. When writing about dying, for instance, it's often better to avoid any mention of tears or crying, as it's so hard to write about the act of crying without using stale or sloppy language. 'Rivers of tears gushed down my face' or 'Tears came to my eyes and I sobbed as though my heart would break' or 'My eyes overflowed with tears.' None of these is going to cut it with your readers.

Perhaps oddly, writing about someone trying not to cry tends to be more moving than writing about someone who is crying.

Writing is more effective when you can illuminate elements of life of which people are unconsciously aware; that they haven't consciously noticed. Usually when people write fictitious accounts of sex or death they mention only the excitement (sex) or the grief (death). That's why their accounts ring false. There's much more happening than those two things. When somebody dies, for example, the survivors might feel emotions like anger, fear, confusion, guilt, freedom, relief, shock, happiness. That's a short list; it could easily be extended. It may help you realise why an account of death that only deals in grief will be unsatisfying.

In *Darkness, Be My Friend*, Ellie discovers that her best friend, Corrie, has been killed.

**Corrie's grave was the third of the little mounds of dirt. It had her name and the date of her death on the white cross, nothing else. Tears kept running down my face, but it was just water out of my eyes; I didn't feel I was crying in the way that people normally do. Like, sobbing. It's lucky Lee was holding me though, because I would have just folded into a heap on the ground if he hadn't been. And if I'd gone down, like a sheep in a drought, I don't think I'd have got up again. That's what war does to you. Either kills you in one go or destroys you bit by bit. One way or the other, it gets you ... And then the horror of it hit me. Corrie was my age, my friend, my best, best friend who I'd shared my childhood with. This was Corrie, whose mother found her crying in her bedroom when she was four and when she asked her what was wrong Corrie sobbed, 'Ellie told me to go to my room, and I haven't even done anything wrong!' Corrie, who played school with me, when we used poddy lambs as the students and tried to make the poor stupid things stand in straight lines for their lessons. Corrie, who had conspired with me to be naughty one day in Grade 1, and we threw Eleanor's lunch in the rubbish tin and filled her lunch box with sheep droppings. We got in so much trouble that we were shocked ... And now my best mate was under the earth, under six feet of cold heavy soil, separated from me by six feet and by eternity. How could it be possible? All those futures we discussed, all those plans to share a flat and go to uni, to travel the world together, to get jobs as pilots or jillaroos or teachers or doctors or governesses: in**

none of those plans did we ever consider for a moment that it might end like this. Death wasn't on our agenda. We never mentioned the word. We thought we were indestructible. And what would happen to me now? Our plans had always been for two, but Corrie had left me and I was on my own. I felt like a Siamese twin who'd been amputated from her other half. Sure I had Fi, and sure I loved her dearly, but I hadn't grown up with her the way I had with Corrie.

A girl in South Australia told me how, when she was eight, a boy in her class was killed instantly when struck in the head by a cricket bat. When she heard what had happened she ran to the spot. She said her first thought when she saw him lying on the ground was, 'At least he won't be able to beat me at swimming anymore.' (They had been the two best swimmers in the class.) This is a typical human story. We don't react in obvious and predictable ways. You need to recognise that in your writing.

## SUMMARY

♦ Give your readers new insights into sex and death.

♦ Recognise the complexity of these subjects – avoid stereotypes.

# Psychology

Did curiosity kill the cat? Or is curiosity the secret of success? Maybe that curious cat tracked down a jug of cream or a city of mice.

A writer who lacks curiosity probably won't amount to much. Most writers are curious about people, especially; and it shows in their books. Driven by their curiosity, they often probe deeper into humanity than any surgeon.

Psychology is the science of human behaviour; a way of increasing your insight into those contradictory, baffling, graceful, ugly creatures called human beings.

It's a pity that many schools don't teach psychology, but you might try other ways of learning about it. There are lots of textbooks on the market, some easy, some advanced. Entertaining texts include *Families* by Robin Skynner and John Cleese and *Manwatching* by Desmond Morris. Another way is to read books that aren't specifically written as textbooks but which still raise important psychological issues. These often look at people who are psychologically abnormal, but we learn about normality by reading them. One such is *Dibs* by Virginia Axline, the true story of a severely disturbed five-year-old boy. Or try *Corrupting the Young* or *Resilience* by Moshe and Tessa Lang, easy to read and both funny and moving.

Quite a few novels explore people's psychological makeup too. Try *Ordinary People* by Judith Guest, about a boy who has survived a suicide attempt. *I Never Promised You A Rose Garden* by Hannah Green convincingly explores the life of a schizophrenic girl. Most good novels show psychological insight. Reading them, one can see the depth and subtlety of the writer's understanding of human beings. That's as true of Tolstoy as it is of Roald Dahl, of Jane Austen as it is of Judy Blume. It's one reason I think Virginia

Andrews' books fail: the psychological truth one looks for is just not there.

## SUMMARY

- ◆ Be curious.
- ◆ Become a student of human behaviour.
- ◆ Make sure your characters are psychologically credible.

# Light

It's strange how painters pay so much attention to light, and yet writers so often ignore it – poor writers, that is.

The impressionist painters became students and lovers of light. Monet, for instance, spent three years painting many canvases of Rouen Cathedral to show how different light affected it. In 1895 he exhibited twenty of these paintings, showing the cathedral from dawn to dusk. He painted his waterlily pond hundreds of times, concentrating on its colours and light. It would be an interesting exercise to do something similar with words . . . to describe the same scene half a dozen times, from dawn through to night.

Light is important to us humans. It influences our moods, our perceptions, our energy levels. A face glimpsed among trees, dappled by the shadows and the green-tinged light reflected from the forest, will seem quite different to the same face seen on a beach in hard, dry, sunlight, or in a darkening room at twilight, with the shadows of a venetian blind striped across it like a convict's uniform.

Sometimes a brief reference is enough, as in *The Fall of the House of Usher* by Edgar Allan Poe:

**Feeble gleams of encrimsoned light made their way through the trellised panes . . .**

or in Jennifer Johnston's *Shadows On Our Skin*:

**Lights from the shop windows made patterns on the wet roads.**

and in *Lord of the Flies* by William Golding:

**. . . there was a scatter of pearly light from the sky down through the trees.**

Sometimes an extended description is needed to set a scene.

This is from *A High Wind in Jamaica* by Richard Hughes:

**The suffused brilliance of the stars lit up everything close quite plainly, but showed nothing in the distance. The black masts towered up, clear against the jewelry (sic), which seemed to swing slowly a little to one side, a little to the other, of their tapering points. The sails, the shadows in their curves all diffused away, seemed flat. The halyards and topping-lifts and braces showed here, were invisible there, with an arbitrariness which took from them all meaning as mechanism.**

**Looking forward with the glowing binnacle light at one's back, the narrow milky deck sloped up to the foreshortened tilt of the bowsprit, which seemed to be trying to point at a single enlarged star just above the horizon.**

And of course light can be used symbolically. In the extract from Joseph Conrad's *Heart of Darkness* which follows, the suggestion is made that although the narrator is surrounded by corruption and evil, it has not yet succeeded in corrupting him:

**The long shadows of the forest had slipped down hill while we talked, had gone far beyond the ruined hovel, beyond the symbolic row of stakes. All this was in the gloom while we down there were yet in the sunshine, and the stretch of the river abreast of the clearing glittered in a still and dazzling splendour, with a murky and overshadowed bend above and below.**

Here the little boy Billy, in *Kes* by Barry Hines, is searching for his kestrel and moves deeper and deeper into the symbolic darkness of despair:

**It was immediately darker, and he had to move with his arms forward to protect his face from the branches of the saplings. Above the saplings were the dark bunches of the**

**hawthorns, and high above these the branches of the tallest trees formed lattice work against the sky.**

In writing a ghost story most people would be sure to include lots of descriptions of light and darkness. But not many people consider it when writing in other genres. Don't be photophobic when you write!

## SUMMARY

♦ Describe light to give a sense of atmosphere to a scene.

♦ Use light symbolically when appropriate.

# Pacing

Imagine a race caller describing the start of the Melbourne Cup. Suppose that as the barriers open he's already screaming at full volume into his microphone:

**AND THEY'RE RACING. OH, FANTASTIC START! OH LOOK AT MAGIC CIRCLE, LEADING ALREADY BY HALF A LENGTH FROM MEXICAN MISS, BUT HERE COMES MEXICAN MISS NOW, SHE'S GETTING TO HIM, MAGIC CIRCLE ON THE RAILS LEADS BY A LONG HEAD, MEXICAN MISS IS WEARING HIM DOWN, JUST A HEAD IN IT NOW, MEXICAN MISS ON THE OUTSIDE, MAGIC CIRCLE HANGING ON, MEXICAN MISS COMING AT HIM, SHE DRAWS LEVEL, MEXICAN MISS, MAGIC CIRCLE, MEXICAN MISS, OH YES, MEXICAN MISS, IT'S MEXICAN MISS, SHE GOES TO THE LEAD, SHE LEADS HALF A LENGTH AT THE 3000, BUT LOOK AT THIS, HERE COMES PIRATE MAN TO CHALLENGE, PIRATE MAN, ON THE OUTSIDE, HE THROWS DOWN THE CHALLENGE . . .**

Yes, you heard right, the 3000. They've gone 200 metres and they've got 3000 still to go. This race caller has a big problem. How can he maintain that level of excitement for another three minutes? Why should he anyway? The early and middle parts of the race generally don't merit that kind of hysteria. But how can he now induce tension and excitement in his listeners when it counts, at the other end of the race? He's left himself nowhere to go. He's got nothing left for the climax.

Writers often make the same mistake.

Every story, every film, has to be paced so that there are lulls and climaxes. If you try to write at full throttle for the whole story: well, it's like trying to race a motorbike at full throttle for too long. Nasty things happen. Nasty oily smelly smoky things.

Movie-makers understand this. Even movies that appear to run at full throttle, like the *Indiana Jones, Terminator, Die Hard* and *Lethal Weapon* movies, actually don't. They have quiet times, long conversations, romantic moments or humorous interludes.

You can of course have more than one climax in a story. You can have more than one climax in a horse race if there's a fall, or severe interference for example. A story, if graphed, can look like this:

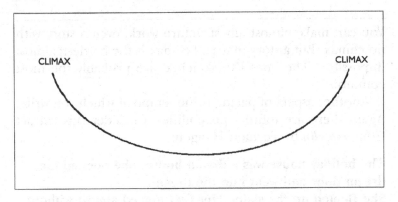

or this:

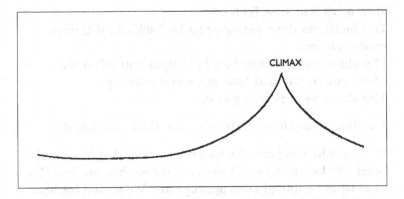

or this:

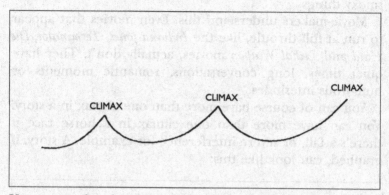

You can make almost any structure work, even a story with no climax. But a story that's all climax is the hardest; almost impossible. The ones I've sketched are probably the most common.

Another aspect of pacing is the tempo at which you write. Again there are infinite possibilities. Consider this extract from *Zeppelin* by Tormod Haugen:

**The holiday house was a dream house. She opened the dream door and went into the dream.**
**She floated up the stairs. Her feet moved almost without touching the ground.**
**Slow arms and slow feet.**
**The bedroom door swung open by itself. As if it were ready for her.**
**The shoes were waiting in a blue light that filled the whole room. She had blue arms and blue legs.**
**The shoes were pointing at her.**

And this from Helen Garner's 'The Dark, the Light':

**We heard he was back. We heard he was staying in a swanky hotel. We heard she was American. We washed our hair. We wore what we thought was appropriate. We waited for him to declare himself. We waited for him to call.**

**No calls came. We discussed his possible whereabouts, the meaning of his silence, the possibilities of his future.**

**We thought we saw him getting into a taxi outside the Rialto, outside the Windsor, outside the Regent, outside the Wentworth, outside the Stock Exchange, outside the Diorama. Was it him? What was he wearing? What did he have on?**

Tempo depends on fashion to some extent. The fashion in past centuries was generally for slower tempos, as you can see in *Tristram Shandy* by Lawrence Sterne:

**In the beginning of the last chapter I informed you exactly when I was born; but I did not inform you how. No, that particular was reserved entirely for a chapter by itself; – besides, Sir, as you and I are in a manner perfect strangers to each other, it would not have been proper to have let you into too many circumstances relating to myself all at once. You must have a little patience. I have undertaken, you see, to write not only my life, but my opinions also; hoping and expecting that your knowledge of my character, and of what kind of mortal I am, by the one, would give you a better relish for the other: As you proceed farther with me, the slight acquaintance, which is now beginning betwixt us, will grow into familiarity; and that, unless one of us is in fault, will terminate in friendship.**

The tempo you choose will depend on the subject matter, your style and your personality. There's a story about Helen Garner sending a postcard to Manning Clark: 'Dear Manning, I'm sick of my style. I want to change it.' He sent a postcard back: 'Dear Helen, your style will not change until you do.'

One way of establishing the correct tempo for your writing is to get a tape of you talking casually with friends or family. Listen for the rhythms and tempo of your speech, then try to reproduce them when you write. Try experimenting, too. Write a description of someone fishing for hours on a hot afternoon without catching anything, but write it in quick tempo. Write a description of a gunfight in very slow tempo. The moment of impact in a car crash is another good one to do in slow tempo. You can make these work if you're a good enough stylist.

One tip from film director Robert Wise, who made *West Side Story*, *The Sound of Music*, and *Star Trek*, *the Motion Picture*: 'If a scene seems a trifle slow as you're filming it, you can bet it'll be twice as slow on the screen.' The same applies to writing and reading.

## SUMMARY

- ◆ Don't write at full throttle.
- ◆ Place climaxes judiciously.
- ◆ Experiment with tempo until you find what suits you and the story.

# Characterisation and Voice

Everyone has a different approach to writing. For me, the single most important thing is to get the voice of the characters. Once I've got that I can usually start writing the book, even if I don't know much else. I might have only the vaguest idea of the plot, the setting and the factual details of the character's life. But if I know how they talk, if I know the words they use and the rhythms and patterns of their speech, if I can hear their voice, then I'm ready to hit the word-processor.

Famous actor Laurence Olivier often talked about the walk of his characters. 'All I care about is the walk,' he said. 'If I've got the walk, the rest follows.'

For Olivier the walk, for me the talk.

When you write as yourself – for example, a History essay or a literature essay or a letter – your voice should be heard clearly. Express yourself in words that are right for you. Don't use the voice of a middle-aged person if you're not middle-aged:

**I hope she fulfils all her expectations in her chosen field of study.**

This was part of a speech I heard in a country high school, when the school vice-captain was farewelling the captain, who was leaving for America. Similarly, when Queen Elizabeth II visited Parkes, NSW, a Year 11 student gave a welcoming speech:

**Your visit will linger forever in our minds.**

A Year 12 boy in Sydney, writing in his school magazine:

... we must all make the little effort that is needed to keep our uniforms neat and tidy and behave in a manner that will surely give the school a reputation of fostering responsible, well-disciplined and courteous young members of society.

That was written in 1993, not 1893. It's the voice of a parent or a teacher, not of a seventeen-year-old.

One of my first jobs was at the Water Board in Sydney. I was assigned to the Personnel Department – now called Human Resources no doubt – and I spent three weeks going through job applications, removing original documents and shredding what was left. There were thousands of applications and it was a pretty boring job, so I started reading the letters as I shredded them. Before long their dullness and repetition began to grind away at my mind, like listening to someone singing the same song over and over:

**Dear Mr Macdonald,**

**I am writing to apply for the position advertised in the *Sydney Morning Herald* on April 15. My name is Melanie Scott and I am a Year 12 student at St Anne's High School. I am studying English, Economics, Physics, Biology and Indonesian. My interests are hockey, water-skiing, reading and music. The reason I think this job would suit me is because I have always liked ...**

Yuk. No wonder Melanie got an equally dull letter back thanking her for her application but informing her that the position had been filled by someone else.

If eighty people apply for the one position, and your letter is like seventy-nine others in the pile, why should an employer hire you? Your letter has to be such that when the employer gets to the bottom of the pile, yours will be the one that sticks in his or her mind.

How can you achieve this? By the end of the three weeks

at the Water Board there were a few letters that stuck in my mind. They stayed there because they were warm and personal; they were sincere, even passionate; they used humour; they struck a confident note; they engaged me as a reader. I felt the personality of the writer in every line, and I liked their personalities: I would have liked to meet those people and get to know them better.

That's personal voice.

John Kirkbride wrote a couple of quirky novels about job applications. The first is called *In Reply to Your Advertisement* and its sequel is called *Thank You for Your Application.* You might enjoy them.

When you speak or write for yourself, don't slip into false or imitative language. We've seen enough hypocritical language over the centuries. There's no need for you to add to it.

I collect examples of authentic personal voice, including the Tracey Wickham statement on swimming quoted earlier. Here's an example from a boarding school in England, where a girl who was sick of the conversation of the horse-lovers around her put up this sign in her corner of the dormitory:

**NO HORSES OR PONIES BEYOND THIS POINT;**
**or they'll be sausages.**
**NO soppy horse or pony talk.**
**NO pathetic photos of 'Honey', 'Midnight', or 'Stardust'**
**etc.**
**NO music apart from Van Halen, Andrew Lloyd Webber**
**and 'Me and My Girl' and Sixties. YEAH!**
**NO breaking wind.**
**NO adults.**
**HORSE HATERS WELCOME.**

I found a note in a Sydney classroom which began:

**Jodie just walked past and bitched at me. What's up her nose?**

Here's an eleven-year-old quoted in the *Age* newspaper, describing her parents' separation:

**When Mum first left I wanted to chop everything up and chuck everything over the floor. I was mad and I didn't eat anything for a day or so. I remember trying to starve myself. I said to Dad, 'I don't want to see Mum again.' And then when I saw her I ran up to her and said, 'Mummy, I want to live with you.' She said, 'You can't darling. Dad wants you, he loves you too much.' And so I said, 'I guess so,' and walked back.**

These last three examples are unmistakably authentic. They show clearly at least one factor in voice: the influence of age. Teenagers have a different voice to children; middle-aged and old people are different again. A school principal probably won't start an assembly with the words: 'Love ya dudes! How's it all hanging?'

What else affects voice? Gender, for sure. Men have always had different voices to women. 'Mate' was a male word in Australia for nearly two hundred years, but women have been using it since about 1970. Words like 'sweet' and 'cute' have traditionally been female words, but it depends on the context: I can say 'This jam's too sweet', but I wouldn't feel comfortable saying 'You're a really sweet bloke.'

Personality and status are probably the biggest determinants of voice. You might remember the Anthony Browne book *Willie the Wimp*. Willie has the bad habit of apologising for everything. When he walks into a lamppost he apologises to the lamppost. He's low status and it shows. High status can be pompous ('It has come to my attention that some of your recent behaviour ...') or aggressive ('You can get stuffed mate') or confident ('Put it there thanks'). High status people often use long words and long sentences, because they know that they won't be interrupted.

When you're writing fiction, all characters must have a distinctive personal voice, so that the reader can believe in them as real people. That's easier if one character is, say, a school principal and the other a teenager, than if they're all school principals or all teenagers. But whatever, it can be done, sometimes by the comparatively easy trick of using speech mannerisms. Samuel Weller, from Charles Dickens's *Pickwick Papers*, pronounces his 'w's as 'v's and his 'v's as 'w's. He was so successful as a literary creation that his appearance in the book, which was published as a serial, sent its sales from fifty copies a month to forty thousand:

**... and he'd go home and laugh till the pig tail wibrated like the penderlum of a Dutch clock. At last, one day the old gen'l'm'n was a-rollin' along, and he sees a pickpocket as he know'd by sight, a-comin' up, arm in arm with a little boy with a wery large head ...**

Sometimes the character is given a word or phrase which she or he uses habitually. I mentioned the repulsive Uriah Heep from *David Copperfield* before. One of his most memorable characteristics was his use of the word 'umble', which grates on the reader more each time he uses it. That single word is probably the main reason people remember Uriah so strongly, over a hundred years after the book was written. His mother was as bad:

**'My Uriah,' said Mrs Heep, 'has looked forward to this, Sir, a long while. He had his fears that our umbleness stood in the way, and I joined in them myself. Umble we are, umble we have been, and umble we shall ever be,' said Mrs Heep.**

Sometimes a character's voice is established by speech rhythms, as in this extract from *Little House on the Prairie* by Laura Ingalls Wilder:

'It rests heavy on my mind,' said Santa Claus. 'They are both of them sweet, pretty, good little things, and I know they are expecting me. I surely do hate to disappoint two good little girls like them. Yet with the water up the way it is, I can't ever make it across that creek. I can figure no way whatsoever to get to their cabin this year. Edwards, would you do me the favour to fetch them their gifts this one time?'

By contrast, here's a black American perspective on the same man; a poem called 'Santa Claws' by Ted Joans:

IF THAT WHITE MOTHER HUBBARD COMES DOWN
MY BLACK CHIMNEY DRAGGING HIS PLAYFUL BAG
IF THAT RED SUITED FAGGOT STARTS HO HO
HOING ON MY ROOFTOP
IF THAT OLD FAT CRACKER CREEPS INTO MY
HOUSE
IF THAT ANTIQUE REINDEER RAPER RACES ACROSS
MY LAWN
IF THAT OLD TIME NIGGER KNOCKER FILLS MY
WIFE'S STOCKING
IF THAT HAINT WHO THINKS HE'S A SAINT COMES
SLED FLYING ACROSS MY HOME
IF THAT OLD CON MAN COMES ON WITH HIS
TOYFUL JIVE
IF THAT OVERSTUFFED GUT BUSTING GANGSTER
SHOWS UP TONIGHT
HE AND ME SHOW GONNA HAVE A BATTLING XMAS
AND IT SHOW AINT GONNA BE WHITE

Only a black American could have written that poem; the rhythms are uniquely of that culture.

Personal voice can also be established by the choice of appropriate vocabulary. This is clearly a teacher:

'We have been talking,' said Penny, 'about ourselves and our personal histories ... Come on, Mick. I'm grateful

**that you're on time but I'd appreciate it if I had your complete attention.'**

That's from Libby Gleeson's *Dodger*. Even if I hadn't told you that Penny was a teacher, you'd have been able to work it out. And that's the test of personal voice. If you've created it successfully, the reader will be able to deduce a lot about the characters just from the words you've put in their mouths. From Penny's short speech we can tell that she is a teacher with a contemporary approach; that the book in fact is set in contemporary times. In the 1950s, for example, she might have said, 'Mick! Pay attention!' or even, 'Jamieson! Get out the front!'

The content of the lesson suggests modern times too.

As a person, Penny seems to be firm but not aggressive or confrontational. A weaker teacher might say, 'Oh come on, Mick, you're spoiling it for everyone', or 'Mick, if you don't pay attention I'm going to have to send you to the office again.' Penny's probably a good teacher.

The first exchange between husband and wife Stanley and Stella in the Tennessee Williams play *A Streetcar Named Desire* tells us almost everything about them and their relationship:

**STANLEY** (*bellowing*): **Hey, there! Stella, Baby! ...**
**STELLA** (*mildly*): **Don't holler at me like that. Hi, Mitch.**
**STANLEY: Catch!**
**STELLA: What?**
**STANLEY: Meat!**
**(He heaves the package at her. She cries out in protest but manages to catch it: then she laughs breathlessly. Her husband and his companion have already started back around the corner.)**
**STELLA** (*calling after him*): **Stanley! Where are you going?**
**STANLEY: Bowling!**
**STELLA: Can I come watch?**
**STANLEY: Come on. (*He goes out.*)**

Stanley has nine words and Stella eighteen. But that's all Williams needs to convey a good sense of their personalities.

If you've done your job properly, by the end of the story the reader should know more about the character than the character knows about himself. Thus, in Oliver Goldsmith's *Vicar of Wakefield* we realise, as we read the Vicar's words, that he is extremely naive. But he never realises that.

**I set him down in my own mind for nothing less than a parliament-man at least; and was almost confirmed in my conjectures when, upon asking what there was in the house for supper, he insisted that the player and I should sup with him at his house, with which request, after some entreaties, we were prevailed on to comply.**

**The house where we were to be entertained lying at a small distance from the village, our inviter observed that, as the coach was not ready, he would conduct us on foot, and we soon arrived at one of the most magnificent mansions I had seen in that part of the country. The apartment into which we were shown was perfectly elegant and modern; he went to give orders for supper, while the player, with a wink, observed that we were perfectly in luck.**

Sadly, it emerges later that their host is the butler, pretending to be the owner of the house while the true owner is away.

In George and Weedon Grossmith's *Diary of a Nobody* Charles Pooter in his diary, reveals himself to be a humorless bore.

**At the office, the new and very young clerk Pitt, who was very impudent to me a week or so ago, was late again. I told him it would be my duty to inform Mr Perkupp, the principal. To my surprise, Pitt apologised most humbly and in a most gentlemanly role. I was unfeignedly pleased to notice this improvement in his manner towards me, and told him I would look over (sic) his unpunctuality. Passing**

down the room an hour later, I received a hard smack in the face from a rolled-up ball of hard foolscap. I turned round sharply, but all the clerks were apparently riveted to their work. I am not a rich man, but I would give half-a-sovereign to know whether that was thrown by accident or design.

The humour derives from his complete lack of awareness of his own pomposity: he never works out that every other character in the book, not to mention the readers, are laughing at him from start to finish. And this is all achieved by the author putting words in the character's own mouth!

Here are some lines from Judy Blume's *Tiger Eyes*. In each case you should be able to tell the age of the speaker and maybe some more information:

'I'm not really feeling up to a party.'
'Nonsense,' Walter says. 'It will do you good.'

'Basically . . . your duties are to assist the nurses and the aides. You'll be delivering mail and flowers . . .'

'But you're my only friend,' she cries, 'and I'm never going to see you again.'

'Safety first, Davey,' Bitsy says. 'Just don't forget it again. We're trying to take good care of you but you've got to help us.'

'Crying is for babies,' he mumbles.

## SUMMARY

- ◆ When you're writing non-fiction, use your own voice.
- ◆ When you're writing fiction, give each significant character an identifiable personal voice.

♦ The words you put in a character's mouth should reveal a lot about that person to the reader ... even more about the character than the character knows about herself.

# Characters in Conflict

Gertrude Stein, an American writer who lived most of her life in Paris, told the French artist Matisse that his work had lost interest for her. She said: 'There is nothing within you that fights itself.' That is a comment of almost uncanny perception. As in art, so in writing. If you want to write great fiction you should use the energy generated by the forces within you that fight each other. But to go further: the most interesting characters to write about are the ones who are in conflict. That can be external conflict: they can be competing in sport, arguing with family or friends or authority figures, fighting in a war, battling the legal system or trying to defeat criminals. One person fighting a large number of people, one person standing against the crowd, is usually attractive, in novels anyway. In real life most of us are angered by the defiant individual.

Status gives lots of opportunities for conflict.

Conflict can of course be internal too: temptation fighting conscience, courage struggling with cowardice, sexual yearnings tempered by fear, greed toe-to-toe with guilt. There are lots of possibilities there. You could write a whole novel about nothing but internal conflict, but a novel with only external conflict would be boring.

This is vital: if you neglect the forces within your characters that are fighting each other, your characters will be of no interest.

Your characters must also evolve during the story. They must change. The way they change will provide the story with much of its tension. Their conflicts may be resolved or exacerbated, or may change in their nature. But if any of the characters are the same at the end of the story as they were at the beginning, you can kiss that Nobel Prize goodbye. How do you feel about a career in dentistry?

## SUMMARY

♦ Characters must be involved in internal conflict and can be involved in external conflict too.

♦ Characters must change as the story progresses.

# Putting Flesh on Bones

What are the first things you want to know about someone when you meet them? In those first five minutes, most people go through a process of trying to put the other person into categories, so they can feel more comfortable with them. After all, the better we know someone the less we fear them. So a lot of questions and answers are often exchanged as we try to fit the person into our existing frameworks. What kind of work do they do? What course are they doing, or what school do they attend? Where do they live? Do you have mutual friends?

But this process starts before you meet. It begins as someone comes towards you. What do you notice first, when the person's still a hundred or more metres away? Gender, race, clothing, size, appearance, approximate age? A lot of this happens unconsciously, but it happens.

The process may help you to get to know the person, but it can also lead you into traps. The danger is that you'll assume the person fits into the stereotypes you hold. They have five rings in each ear? They're wild. They live in a certain suburb? They're rich. They're old? They're conservative. There is some truth in most stereotypes; otherwise the stereotypes would never have evolved. But it's naive and short-sighted to rely on them. We think we're getting to know the person but we may be dangerously wrong.

One of my early jobs was in Sydney Hospital Casualty. One busy night I was standing in the corridor with a doctor and nurse when a striking young woman came towards us. She wore red leather hot pants, walked on tall heels and had a huge mass of fluffy pink hair. 'My God,' the nurse muttered to us, 'look what's coming into Casualty now.' The doctor gave her a puzzled look but said nothing until the woman reached us. Then he turned to the nurse. 'I'd like you to meet my fiancee,' he said quietly.

It was a nice moment.

When creating characters for a piece of fiction you need to establish many of the same things that matter when you meet real people: gender, age, appearance, dress, race and occupation. But don't have the characters conforming to all the stereotypes. The interest people have for us is often in direct proportion to the degree in which they vary from the stereotypes. A stockman who presses wildflowers, a bishop with a stutter, a dressmaker who writes poetry, a hospital matron who's a hypochondriac ('You think you've got problems!' she says to the patients), a gay professional golfer ... All fiction proceeds by way of contrasts. The contrasts generate energy whenever they rub together. This is as true for characters as it is for plot.

The most important element in creating characters, though, is to give them personality. There are quite a few artificial exercises to help you do this. For example: try designing a bathroom for your character. If you do it in enough detail you should get a good feeling for their personality. Or make a family tree for them, going back several generations, with little notes about each person on it. Or role-play an interview in which you play your character on a TV talk show and someone else plays the interviewer. Or list all their likes and hates – favourite colour and so on. Or write resumes of the three most significant events in their life. Or write a few conversations between your character and some other people, to help establish personal voice. Or draw an abstract self-portrait for your character.

You can tell when a character's become real for you. After you've written the story, go back and try to change the character's name. If you can't do it, then you know you're getting somewhere!

## SUMMARY

◆ Know and show your characters' personalities.

◆ Don't let them conform too closely to stereotypes.

# Background (and Foreground)

Artists pay a lot of attention to background. So do photographers. Do you, when you write?

The background to a story should reflect and enhance what's happening in the foreground.

A couple of years ago I was watching a student doing a drawing assignment. She'd been asked to draw a pair of hands in any position, and she chose to draw them around a throat, throttling it. After she'd done that she started filling in the background. She decided to have the scene in a room, so she drew in a wall, then put a painting hanging on it; a painting of a tree. Watching all this, I thought it time to make a suggestion: that the painting on the wall should reflect what was happening with the hands. She thought for a moment then did something quite brilliant. She sketched a creeper curling around the tree, strangling its trunk. Now her drawing had a depth and unity that it previously lacked; the background reflected the foreground, so the notion of one living thing slowly killing another was presented explicitly and implicitly.

In the best writing we find the same depth and unity. Writers should take as much care with the backgrounds to their stories as they do with the foregrounds. In *Lord of the Flies* we have this, the opening to chapter nine, where William Golding uses the background to convey a sense of impending doom:

**Over the island the build-up of clouds continued. A steady current of heated air rose all day from the mountain and was thrust to ten thousand feet; revolving masses of gas piled up the static until the air was ready to explode. By**

early evening the sun had gone and a brassy glare had taken the place of clear daylight. Even the air that pushed in from the sea was hot and held no refreshment. Colours drained from water and trees and pink surfaces of rock, and the white and brown clouds brooded. Nothing prospered but the flies ...

Throughout *So Much to Tell You* I tried to suggest a sense of things shattering but coming together again, to form a backdrop to Marina's story. I wanted to give readers an awareness that eventually there would be a healing of some kind in Marina's life:

I use grey school blankets but most of the beds are covered by doonas that girls have brought from home, with vivid doona covers. My favourite is Ann Maltin's on the bed opposite me. It looks like a jigsaw of stars: white on a dark background. But it is a jigsaw: none of the stars is complete.

I am always first in bed and I often lie there looking at the fragmented stars, trying to put them together. I suppose Ann must have been watching me doing this. Last night she looked across at me and said: 'They do fit together, but it took me years to figure it out.'

So, we're talking symbols here. Students often want to know if writers use symbols deliberately or if they're just figments of an English teacher's imagination. I use symbols both deliberately and unconsciously. Sometimes I'm startled when I look back over a book to find that my subconscious was writing a whole underlying story of which my conscious mind was not aware. As the subconscious never communicates with us directly, we have to look for symbols to find what it's saying. I mentioned James Barrie before, and his sad obsession with his brother who died when only thirteen. Barrie's books are full of characters who never grow old. In his play Mary Rose the eponymous character goes missing for twenty-five years on a mysterious island, where she is frozen in time. When she returns her family has grown old but she has not aged a day. Even before this, although she's a married woman with a child, she is so immature that she really is a child herself. Barrie has found two different ways to keep her young forever. For example, her mother says:

**Simon, I am very anxious to be honest with you. I have sometimes thought that our girl is curiously young for her age – as if – you know how just a touch of frost may stop the growth of a plant and yet leave it blooming. It has sometimes seemed to me as if a cold finger had once touched my Mary Rose.**

Here's a stage direction:

**Mary Rose is sitting demure but gay, holding her tongue with her fingers, like a child.**

In Barrie's *Peter Pan* Peter says:

**'Wendy, I ran away the day I was born ... It was because I heard father and mother,' he explained in a low voice, 'talking about what I was to be when I became a man.' He was extraordinarily agitated now. 'I don't want ever to be a man,' he said with passion. 'I want always to be a little boy and to have fun ...'**

And later:

**'Long ago,' he said, 'I thought like you that my mother would always keep the window open for me; so I stayed away for moons and moons and moons, and then flew back; but the window was barred, for mother had forgotten all about me, and there was another little boy sleeping in my bed.'**

It does seem that Barrie had little understanding of the symbolism for him of these characters with arrested developments. Eighteen years after writing *Peter Pan* he jotted in his notebook: 'It is as if long after writing "P. Pan" its true meaning came to me. Desperate attempt to grow up but can't.' (Quoted in *J. M. Barrie and the Lost Boys* by Andrew Birkin.)

Some years ago I taught a girl who had an Italian Australian boyfriend. One day this girl showed her best friend and me an account of a dream she'd had. She said she was puzzled by it and wanted to know its meaning. We both read it and laughed, unable to believe that she was not aware of its sexual implications. But she wasn't. The dream is a perfect example of the subconscious communicating through symbols that aren't consciously understood or appreciated:

**I'm not too sure where I was or how I got there but I had a big beautiful brown horse with a shimmering coat and the softest eyes. He talked to me and instead of me riding on its back I wrapped my legs around its neck or front legs or somewhere and held its neck so we could talk face to face. I don't know whether it was male or female but I will have it male because I don't like calling horses 'it'. We went galloping everywhere and I felt completely safe and at ease while I was leaning against his front and I could feel the muscles of his front legs moving. I think we even did some jumps which is strange because I can't ride well at all. We had a deadline to meet but I don't know who it was with – someone important to do with school or education. We were pushed for time and then got caught in some barbwire but we got out. I can't remember much else but it was the most beautiful horse I've ever seen. God it was stunning.**

I think the references to deadlines 'to do with school', and the barbed wire, were related to the pressure she and her boyfriend were suffering from teachers wanting to end their relationship.

Your subconscious controls most of your body language.

It can take over almost completely when the conscious mind is drunk, drugged, hypnotised or, as we've seen, asleep. We see flashes of it when we make mistakes, hence the expression 'Freudian slips' for mistakes which are not mistakes but are really glimpses into the subconscious. In 1997 North Melbourne footballer Wayne Schwass was suspended during the finals for foul play. The next day, protesting his innocence during an interview on radio station Triple M, he said 'I knew in my heart I was guilty.' 'What did you say?' asked the shocked interviewer. 'Oh, I mean not guilty,' Schwass replied, suddenly realising his mistake. A slip like that suggests that he didn't have a very clear conscience about the incident that led to his suspension.

In 1997 an American right wing TV host, commenting on women weightlifters, remarked: 'I like my men soft and fluffy,' then was overwhelmed with embarrassment as he realised what he'd said. Perceptive viewers were left wondering about his private life.

When you write a story, the times when your subconscious are most likely to be writing a subtext for you are when you're intensely emotionally involved or when you're tired, under great pressure or feeling in a 'dream-like' state. If you can find pieces of writing you've done under those circumstances, have another look at them. You might be startled at symbols you've used unknowingly. You might learn something about yourself!

Here's a paragraph from one such piece of writing by a fourteen-year-old girl. Can you interpret the subtext?

**In another corner of the ground my grandmother was picking some blue and purple flowers. I watched her intently as she threaded them together and completing (sic) places them on my head. I thanked her. Breathless because of her kindness and thoughtfulness I turned in another direction where a large tree was standing outstretched. I moved towards it and started to climb. The**

bark was rough against my legs and I cried out in pain but feeling the need to climb it I continued. I knew the tree was trying to protect something but I was not sure what. One more branch led me to the top where I saw hidden four tiny blue and white speckled eggs. I cried out to my grandmother but she warned me not to touch them. Although I was disappointed for I so much wanted to caress the eggs I returned to the ground.

At other times writers choose symbols deliberately. When I do that I don't care if the readers notice them consciously. I think they enrich the text in a subtle way and add depth to the reader's understanding of what's happening. Here, in *Take My Word for It*, Lisa writes of a childhood toy:

Last time Chloe rang I asked her to look for my old ballerina box when she went to Mt Sandon. It's nothing much – just a tacky old music box that has a dancing ballerina when you open the lid. But when I was a kid I thought it was the greatest thing I'd ever been given. I'd begged for one for a year, and finally got it for Christmas – I can't remember whether it was from Santa or who. I loved it so much. The trouble is, I was here at school when everything got packed and moved, and so much of my stuff got lost. Maybe it was thrown out, I don't know. Anyway, when I asked Chloe tonight, she said she hadn't had time to look for it. God she's a selfish bitch. It's pathetic of me to want it, I know, but I just do.

The ballerina's stupid when you think about it – the way she just goes round and round.

At the end of the book Lisa talks of people who feel that they're 'stuck on a roundabout'. That's the way she once felt about her own life; hence the significance of the ballerina to her.

Perhaps the most common symbol used in literature and films is the storm, to represent approaching unhappiness for a character or characters. Here is an example from *The Silver Sword* by Ian Serraillier:

**They were so excited that they did not notice how heavy the air was and how dark the clouds ... Suddenly there was a great clap of thunder. It rolled and echoed far away into the distant Swiss mountains.**

Strictly speaking this is part of the plot rather than a symbolic use of weather but in the extract below from *Fahrenheit 451* by Ray Bradbury it's clearly symbolic; signalled to the reader as such:

**You could feel the war getting ready in the sky that night. The way the clouds moved aside and came back, and the way the stars looked, a million of them swimming between the clouds, like the enemy discs, and the feeling that the sky might fall upon the city and turn it to chalk dust, and the moon go up in red fire; that was how the night felt.**

Also in Bradbury's *Something Wicked This Way Comes*:

**At dawn a juggernaut of thunder wheeled over the stony heavens in a spark-throwing tumult.**

And in *The Sweet-Shop Owner* by Graham Swift:

**The needle in the barometer pointed to 'Change'.**

Colours are commonly used: black for death; white for innocence or virginity; red for danger. In the movie of *One Flew Over the Cuckoo's Nest* the first shot of the Big Nurse shows her dressed in black and under a red light. The perceptive viewer will realise from this that the nurse is a figure of danger and death. In Peter Weir's film of *Picnic at Hanging Rock*, the girls who disappear are dressed in virginal white, but the only girl who returns does so in scarlet, the colour of prostitution. Weir is suggesting that she's had a sexual experience of some kind. He reinforces this idea by the many background shots of swans. Swans are a common phallic symbol because of the shape of their necks.

In *Lord of the Flies* the conch shell is the symbol of law and order. It's a big white shell, but as law and order gradually break down on the island, the conch shell becomes more transparent and more frail. When the shell finally shatters we know the kids are in a heap of trouble; it's every boy for himself.

Getting into this kind of writing isn't so hard. These very specific exercises are helpful.

Write about someone who's in a room alone. As you describe the room, include some feature that will give a subtle suggestion that the person is a prisoner. Note: bars on the window are not symbols, nor are they subtle! Bars would be part of the imprisonment. You want something that is not part of the person's imprisonment but which is a little story of imprisonment in itself. A fly in a web would do it, for example. So would a goldfish in a bowl. So would a copy of *The Man in the Iron Mask*.

Describe a person sitting in a car on a long trip. Suggest, by referring to some background object, that the person is heading towards an unpleasant experience.

Describe a first meeting between two people. Include a passing mention of something that symbolically suggests a long loving relationship will develop between them.

## SUMMARY

♦ Pay attention to the background when you write.

♦ Use symbols – the language of the subconscious – to amplify and enrich a story.

♦ Don't block your subconscious if it wants to add a sub text to your story.

# Remember ...

Sit on the floor with a group of people (family or friends are especially good). Get everyone in a circle. Take it in turns to tell a true memory from your life (from an hour ago or ten years ago, whatever). But restrict yourself to one sentence only. Each person must start with the words 'I remember' – that's incredibly, monumentally important. Go round the circle as often as you want, or as often as time allows.

Alternatively, try writing a series of memories, again restricting yourself to one sentence and starting with the words, 'I remember'.

**I remember a yellow squeaking rubber cat we used to have on top of the fridge.**

**I remember the first time I tasted pizza.**

**I remember taking my baby sister to the tops of hills in her pram, letting the pram go, and chasing it down the hills.**

**I remember breaking the window of a factory next door with a cricket ball, and being scared I'd get in trouble, but my parents just laughed and said, 'It must have been a big hit'.**

**I remember breaking my ankle when I fell downhill while splitting logs with a crowbar.**

**I remember trying to stay awake all Christmas Eve to see Santa come down the chimney.**

I remember killing a spider one evening then dreaming about spiders all night.

I remember how racked with fear I was the first time I stood in front of a class as a teacher.

I remember singing, 'Does your chewing gum lose its flavour on the bed-post overnight' to the rest of the class when I was in grade five.

I remember hearing about the Berlin Wall coming down.

I remember eating Choo Choo bars and getting black marks all over my clothes and face.

I remember finding a snake in our cubby when we were in grade six.

I remember going with this girl whose father was a cop, and one night we were in the back of a car going across a bridge, and we realised he was in a police car in the next lane.

I remember when I was about eight, and at the beach, I went into the girls' changing room by mistake.

I remember losing a jumper my grandmother had knitted for me.

I remember my brother educating me about rock'n'roll and how sophisticated I thought he was when he started buying records.

I remember my grandmother's slow death from cancer.

## I remember the thrill of coming sixth in a race, out of two hundred runners.

This is a great way of building up a data bank of material that you can use in writing. Everyone has thousands of stories that can be drawn on if only you can remember them!

# PART THREE

# 600 Writing Topics

# Quickies

1    What's your favourite kitchen appliance, and why?
2    What are three things that could never be photographed?
3    Name four jobs that no-one ever thought of before.
4    List ten uses for dead batteries.
5    Give five ways of stopping a plane when its brakes have failed.
6    What's the most beautiful part of your body? Describe it. What's the ugliest? Describe it.
7    If you had to move, where would you like to live and why?
8    What world record would you most like to break and why?
9    How would you change your school, workplace or local shopping centre, to make it better?
10    Write some questions you would like answered.
11    Which rules are you happy with? Which ones are you unhappy with?
12    What's the most recent advice your parents gave you? What's the best advice they ever gave you? The worst?
13    How much does your appearance tell us about you? (Including clothes.)
14    List ten revolting sandwich fillings.
15    List the world's six most expensive sandwich fillings.
16    Suggest five laws a caveman would need for his family.
17    You find a bicycle in a chimney. Give four explanations of how it came to be there.
18    You've been left a million dollars on condition that you give it away. To whom or what would you give it? Why?
19    Do you usually know when you're acting in a good way? In a bad way? How?
20    You're in a cave with no tools or weapons. A huge

hungry bear is standing in the only opening. Suggest five ways you could get out.

21 Write a menu fit for an enemy.

22 Suggest six ways to get a ping-pong ball out of a (vertical) drain.

23 Was the wheel humanity's greatest invention?

24 Nominate five reasons for liking the place you live in and five reasons for disliking it.

25 Describe how you like to get comfortable.

26 Who's the most repressed group in the world? Justify your answer.

27 If, because of the energy crisis, you're only allowed to keep one electrical appliance, what would it be? Why

28 A train is racing towards a bridge at 120 kilometres an hour. You're outside the train and you know that the bridge has collapsed. Suggest five ways you could stop the train.

29 List three things that are unlikely to be ever made of glass.

30 Suggest ten good writing topics.

31 Write ten ways you could amuse yourself if the TV broke down.

32 Write your own 'odd one out' questions and answer them e.g. popcorn, Queensland, fear, magazine. What's the odd one out and why?

33 Describe a common object without saying what it is.

34 Write the five worst things that adults say to kids.

35 List six bizarre excuses for not doing your homework.

36 List ten ways to cross a crocodile filled river. There's no bridge and you have no tools.

37 What I like and dislike about being Australian (or other nationalities, if appropriate).

38 What I like and dislike about TV.

39 Write down ten wonderful new insulting names for future enemies you might make.

40 What's your favourite tinned food?

41 Write a one-word poem. A two-word poem.
   three ... four ... ten ...

42 You're alone, on a deserted beach. You turn away for
   a moment. When you turn back your towel has gone.
   Give four possible explanations for this.

43 A girl finds two dollars but leaves it on the ground.
   Why?

44 List ten things that go up and down.

45 Write a dinner menu for someone who loves yellow.
   List food and drinks that can be served.

46 Take a boring sentence. Start replacing each word
   with one (or two) new ones.

47 Write five impossibly difficult or strange
   questions.

48 List three big things in your house that you'd be
   prepared to get rid of if you had to make space.

49 Suppose your house burns down. List six ways you
   could turn this into a positive experience.

50 Write three differences between carpet and ice-cream.

51 What seven items would you want to have if you were
   the last person on earth?

52 Write a horoscope for cars.

53 Choose someone else and write down the ways in
   which you're similar to them and the ways in which
   you are different.

54 Write the history of the world in twenty words.

55 Write down all the opposites you can think of. Are
   any of them true?

56 What's the biggest thing you've ever seen? What's the
   smallest?

57 What's the loudest noise you ever made?

58 What's the loudest noise you ever heard?

59 List five ways you pass your time in class when you're
   bored.

60 Write three things that Mars and blackberries have in
   common.

61 'Summer afternoon – summer afternoon; to me those have always been the two most beautiful words in the English language.' (Henry James) What's your favourite pair of words?

62 List your five favourite smells.

63 What picture books did you like most when you were little? What did you like about them?

64 List all the different ways you could annoy your neighbours without having them call the cops.

65 What would you do if you saw someone stealing?

66 How would you feel about your parents adopting a child of a different race?

67 Which kid in the family is it best to be? The oldest? The youngest? Second, third, fourth, tenth? The only one?

68 What's your favourite time of day and why?

69 List seven things our society would be better off without. (Alcohol? The lettuce that prawn cocktails are served in and which no-one ever eats?)

70 What sensible, practical rules for modern manners should we observe?

71 'Bookshops sell more books on Tuesdays than any other days.' Assuming this is true, how many reasons can you think of to explain it?

72 What is the opposite of time and why? The opposite of chocolate? The opposite of camels? The opposite of zero? Of human beings?

73 What was the most memorable party you ever attended and why?

74 Describe a practical joke you've seen or been involved in.

75 Name three things you enjoy doing now that you probably won't enjoy in three years.

76 Name three things that you don't enjoy doing now that you probably will enjoy in three years.

77 Are there any questions you've never asked, for fear of the answer you might get?

**78** Describe your favourite piece of clothing.

**79** Describe boredom.

**80** Describe, to a person born deaf, what speech is.

**81** What's the slowest thing you've ever seen? And the fastest? (Not counting aeroplanes.)

**82** List three questions you would ask if you were guaranteed a totally honest answer. Who would you ask?

**83** List ten imaginative ways to reduce car accidents.

**84** Write a spell that'll make someone get fatter.

**85** Write seven funny things.

**86** Write seven sad things.

**87** Write down a series of random letters then write sentences using each letter as the first letter of each successive word: e.g. AFDSHW: All fat dentists should have wigs.

**88** Write a conversation where someone mentions a type of fish in every sentence. (Adapted from 'Whose Line is it Anyway?')

**89** What questions do adults not know the answers to?

**90** Write seven peaceful things.

**91** Write seven bad things.

**92** What are the best and worst things about being female? About being male?

**93** Write a recipe (like a cake recipe) describing what you'd see as a good time, then write one for a bad time.

# Discursive

**94** List the differences between children and adults.

**95** There's no progress without discontent.

**96** 'Hate is just a failure of the imagination.' (Graham Greene)

**97** 'Friendship first, competition second.' This is, or was, the Chinese approach to sport. Do you think it is a valid approach?

**98** What are the differences between males and females?

**99** Write your thoughts on a controversial topic for ten minutes. Discuss it with someone else for twenty minutes. Write your thoughts about the issue again, for another ten minutes, without re-reading your first piece.

**100** 'Every great advance began in the realm of the fanciful.' (C. G. Jung)

**101** 'Action is the enemy of thought.' (Joseph Conrad)

**102** 'Everyone thinks of changing humanity, and no-one thinks of changing himself.' (Leo Tolstoy)

**103** 'What you do will be insignificant, but it is important that you do it.' (Mahatma Gandhi)

**104** 'All property is theft.' (Karl Marx)

**105** Describe the typical Australian (but beware of stereotypes).

**106** In what circumstances, if any, would you consider it allowable to kill other humans? Justify your answer.

**107** How can you tell if someone's intelligent?

**108** When are people no longer children? How do you tell that they've 'grown up'?

**109** 'In such an ugly age, the true protest is beauty.' So who do you see who's protesting?

**110** 'In order to make a mistake, a man must already

judge in conformity with humanity.' (Ludwig Wittgenstein)

111 Write an account of a trial where 'Youth' is the defendant, and various witnesses are called.

112 'There is enough for everyone's need but not enough for everyone's greed.' (Mahatma Gandhi)

113 'If you want to test a person's character, give him power.' (Abraham Lincoln)

114 'Everyman for himself, and God against all.' (Werner Herzog) Is this the way it is?

115 Take a controversial issue – a personal one of yours, or an issue that affects a lot of people. List all the people you think might have an opinion on this issue, then write what you think their points of view might be.

116 Do Australians have a sense of humour?

117 Has Science killed more people than it has saved?

118 What are your views on punishment?

119 Does suffering have any value?

120 Do we live in a democracy?

121 Write a conversation where one person convinces another to change his/her viewpoint on something.

122 Why do people have children?

123 In what ways do schools curb imagination?

124 'The best way out is always through.' Write a story which proves or disproves the truth of this contention.

125 Write a piece centring on a question of discrimination on the grounds of sexuality. (Dr Ray Misson)

126 Life sucks.

127 Australians prefer dogs to children.

128 'Violence is the way stupid people try to level the playing field.' (*New Yorker* magazine.) Write a story which shows this to be true – or untrue.

129 'If you want to truly understand something, try to change it.' Try changing something, then write about

any new understanding of it that you have gained.

130 'The more furiously someone denies something the more true it is.' Write about a person of whom that is true.

# Based on a Book

131 Interview a character from the book – write it as though it's the transcript of a TV or radio interview.

132 Write a letter to a character in the book.

133 Write a summary of the book for a seven-year-old.

134 Write a scene when a character from the book finds himself/herself in another book you know well.

135 Write a defence for a 'villain', e.g. the wolf in *The Three Little Pigs*, Jack in *Lord of the Flies*.

136 What are the least important parts of the book?

137 Choose a character from the book and write the similarities and differences between you and that character.

138 'The further it's seen to be from people's own understanding, the more evil it's seen to be.' Is this true of situations in the book?

139 How much is this book a story of loss of innocence?

140 How much do changes in the status of the characters give the book tension?

141 Would this book make a good movie? What would need changing? What locations that you personally know of could you use?

142 How much is this book a story of an innocent person finding himself/herself in a situation that is incompatible with innocence?

143 Write a conversation between a character in the book and her/his conscience.

144 Discuss the main relationships in the book.

145 'People who read this book will have more insight – to themselves and their world.' Is this true?

146 How intelligent is the main character in this book?

147 'They chose to destroy because they did not

understand.' Is this true of some characters in this book?

148 Explain how the main character develops as the story proceeds.

149 'It's the story of a person growing, learning, changing.' Is this true of the book?

# Topics for Short Stories

**150** From a window.

**151** An unusual love story.

**152** My life was boring until . . .

**153** Frogs with dirty little lips,
Dirty little warts on their finger tips,
Dirty 'n' green, tiny 'n' mean,
Flopping around the edge of the stream.
(Frank Zappa)

**154** The Teddy Bears' Picnic. (In an offbeat style?)

**155** Write about a game of chess which is more than a game, where black and white pieces represent something – two opposing forces, or armies, maybe.

**156** We shall not cease from exploring
And the end of all our exploring
Will be to arrive where we started
And know the place for the first time
(T. S. Eliot)

**157** Write a conversation in which someone intends to ring their doctor but dials the butcher by mistake.

**158** Would the last person to leave please turn off the lights?

**159** On the outside looking in. (Bindi Thompson)

**160** Confessions of a six-year-old. (Bindi Thompson)

**161** My Degree in Late Night Movies. (Sandy McEwen)

**162** Married in black. (Lynelle Eaves)

**163** ' . . . And when they came home . . . ' (Michele Williams)

**164** Take a fantasy voyage to the great dark unused section of the brain. (Bruce Stevenson)

**165** Nonsense.

**166** Nothing.

**167** K.

168 No.

169 Yes.

170 A beginning.

171 White.

172 Gobble and Munch.

173 World War VIII.

174 Lie utterly motionless for as long as you can, then write a story in which a character has to be utterly motionless for some reason.

175 Describe a fight between a sorillion and a chomwit.

176 He/she chose to destroy, because he/she did not understand.

177 Love's not the way to treat a friend.

178 An entrance, an exit. (Tessa Jones)

179 A science fiction forest.

180 February 30.

181 One person and a crowd.

182 A town called Cloud, California.

183 Shadows.

184 The long and winding road. (The Beatles)

185 I have nearly finished digging my hole.

186 They're selling postcards of the hanging. (Bob Dylan)

187 The world is now open for business.

188 The fool on the hill. (The Beatles)

189 The monster museum.

190 Sunday morning, three a.m.

191 Persuade the devil you're bad enough to be allowed into hell.

192 Born to laugh at tornadoes.

193 'When love comes along, there is no right or wrong, your love is your love.' (West Side Story)

194 Write a story for children in which there's 'lots of food and lots of fighting'. (Norman Lindsay)

195 A public phone is ringing in a deserted street. You pick it up . . .

196 Welcome to my nightmare. (Alice Cooper)

**197** The note that breaks the silence.

**198** Pigs keep clean in washing machines.

**199** Write a journey through a house of horrors which is personalised for you – all your personal bogeymen are there.

**200** I was a victim of Rock'n'Roll.

**201** Invisible friends.

**202** You've got the right string baby, but the wrong yo-yo.

**203** Never stop.

**204** Write the worst story you can possibly write.

**205** I had a dream last night. I dreamed Jesus moved in down the street.

**206** Write about a librarian who tries to discourage people from borrowing books.

**207** A town called Nothing, Texas.

**208** Write a set of nonsense instructions for . . . for what?

**209** Write a modern version of an old legend or a Biblical parable.

**210** The company forgives a moment of madness. (film title)

**211** My mum the bushranger.

**212** The human zoo.

**213** Write a piece set in the future, incorporating one major change from today's world (show us the change: don't tell us what it is).

**214** Piercing noises of the future. (Tim Hibberd)

**215** How I was systematically destroyed by the idiots. (film title)

**216** Blood, dung, honey, oil, water, salt.

**217** The happy-ending machine.

**218** You've had a nasty accident. When you recover from the surgery you find your brain's been transplanted to a body of the opposite sex.

**219** Write a fake essay on a weird subject.

**220** The beast that shouted love at the heart of the world.

221 A tiny spaceship lands on the back of your hand ...

222 'It's not over yet.'

223 Write a story in which people die in very strange ways.

224 No-one suffers like the mechanic.

225 'I don't believe in kindly humour. I don't think it exists.' (S. J. Perelman) Write a humorous piece that's cruel. Write one that isn't.

226 Write a prayer for the twenty-first century.

227 I was cured by Rock'n'Roll.

228 Describe tomorrow.

229 Write a story beginning 'Once below a time ... '

230 Invent a story telling how some things were invented – roast turkey, laughing gas, fireworks, clothes.

231 Describe a visit to the dream factory.

232 Nothing else matters.

233 Write about the death of an animal.

234 Describe a group of humans who have a lot of time on their hands.

235 Write a piece where the end of the story is told at the beginning.

236 Catch a train that takes you into a strange land.

237 Beyond belief.

238 'That's what's wrong with this place!'

239 Write the transcript of a completely chaotic TV newscast.

240 Write a story in which you exaggerate everything.

241 Write a story about someone who's very controlled on the outside but out of control on the inside.

242 Describe a meal at your place as though a sporting commentator's broadcasting it.

243 Rimmed by uncertainty.

244 Write a story such that you're astonished by your own daring.

245 Evil.

246 Take a motorbike journey through time.

**247** Write a piece in which an object binds the story together.

**248** 'What I didn't do on my holidays.'

**249** A bedtime story for a young vampire.

**250** Use this ending: 'And they all lived unhappily ever after.'

**251** Write a story in which you, the author, intervene in the story at some point ... you walk into the story.

**252** Keep on going till it all stops flowing.

**253** This is the way the world ends
This is the way the world ends,
This is the way the world ends,
Not with a bang, but a whimper.
(T. S. Eliot)

**254** 'Just one minute more.'

**255** The only weed in the garden. (Tessa Jones)

**256** Do I dare disturb the universe?

**257** No name in the street.

**258** I looked the other way, pretending to smile.

**259** I never thought this would happen to me!

**260** Bye now, Camille, take care of yourself.

**261** Why?

**262** The masked poet.

**263** The seventh daughter.

**264** A true story.

**265** The swimmer.

**266** Awakening to the terror of the same old day. (Harvey Pekar)

**267** The good soldier.

**268** And the Lord said, 'Let there be hamsters.'

**269** The straight and narrow.

**270** Things that go bump in the night.

**271** Write a piece from the point of view of someone evil.

**272** Write an episode from the childhood of a famous person ... e.g. Adolf Hitler, Princess Diana.

273 'It's easier to be angry than sad.' Write a story about a character who finds it easier to be angry than sad.

274 Write a story in which the first part describes a life as it then was, the second part describes a life as it now is.

275 'In the beginning was a void, guarded by seven spirits . . .'

276 Write a piece from the point of view of someone who is only half human.

277 'Show me a hero and I'll write you a tragedy.' You write that story.

278 You have a magic button on your shirt. Every time you twist it . . .

279 Write a story in which the songs that come on the radio reflect what's happening to the character at that moment in the story.

280 'I'm looking at the river but I'm dreaming of the sea.' Randy Newman. Write about someone in a comparable situation.

281 Write about a family where the child bullies the parents. It could be a humorous piece, but may not be.

282 Write a diary account of someone's day, five minutes at a time (i.e. an entry every five minutes), fiction or non-fiction.

283 Rewrite an ancient Creation story (e.g. the garden of Eden) in modern poetic English.

284 Take some words that sound interesting – slurp, muffin, avocado, gonorrhea, pooch – and use them in a story, but with new meanings that you've assigned to them.

285 Write a diary of a boring person.

286 'All beauty is transient.' Write a story where the poignancy of this observation is illustrated.

287 A Christmas story: Santa recounts some incidents from his travels.

**288** 'An innocent abroad' is the theme of many books and films – *Crocodile Dundee* for example. Write your own innocent abroad story.

**289** 'I came from nowhere and made something out of my life, and you came from somewhere and are trying to make nothing out of yours.' (Line from a movie.) Write a story about two people of whom this could be said.

**290** 'If you ignore your children they'll make themselves known somehow.' Write a story about a child in this situation.

**291** Write a story about house cats, that have gone wild and grown to a large size.

**292** 'The last time I saw him/her ...' It's an infallible opening line!

**293** Write about a human being who has a relationship with a machine.

**294** A wild animal from your dreams becomes 'real' – can you tame it?

**295** Write about a school for bad boys and girls. A good boy or girl goes there, and won't conform. What happens to him or her? Does he/she get expelled?

**296** Robin Hood and her Merry Women.

**297** You wake up and find you have a new scar on your body ...

**298** You come home and find the house is empty; your parents appear to have moved away, and taken everything with them. You don't trust your neighbours, so you don't want to go to them ...

**299** Write a story in which there's forgiveness for a terrible crime.

**300** Write about someone with a secret.

**301** Sadness.

**302** Take some little idea that looks like fun, and turn it into a story. (This is supposed to be how Walt Disney generated his movies.)

**303** Reinvent the 1788 invasion of Australia: write a story in which a shipload of Aborigines arrive off the coast of Australia and take possession of it from its strange Anglo inhabitants.

**304** Write a 'choose your own adventure' story set in a contemporary environment, like a school or a suburban street. Be funny. Be really funny. (Try doing it on a huge wall chart.)

**305** Write a fortunately/unfortunately story: 'Fortunately I won a two-week holiday in Japan. Unfortunately I hate flying. Fortunately there was a fishing boat going that way and I got a lift. Unfortunately . . .'

**306** Write a monologue where someone slowly turns into a dog. (Adapted from 'Whose Line is it Anyway?')

**307** Write a piece that makes fun of someone who's obsessed with their own health.

# Poetry

**308** Write a 'sick in bed poem', describing your feelings at being confined to bed by illness.

**309** Write a poem in the form of a letter, beginning 'Dear . . .'

**310** Write a poem that will persuade someone to do something or to believe something.

**311** Write a poem that begins 'These have I loved.' (See 'The Great Lover' by Rupert Brooke.)

**312** Write a poem about love in which the word love is not mentioned.

**313** Write a poem in which every line begins with the word 'Now'.

**314** Write a poem that describes something or someone (you, perhaps) as it is on the outside and as it is on the inside.

**315** Write a poem about the end of the world.

**316** Write a poem that describes the different things you dream of.

**317** Write a poem that begins 'Let there be peace, and let it begin with me.'

**318** Write a poem explaining how difficult it is to live your life.

**319** Take one interesting word and write a poem that describes it.

**320** Start a poem with a line of dialogue.

**321** Write a poem in which each line is a lie.

**322** **The Cello**
To tell you
the truth
I never
wanted to be
a cello.

> When I was
> wood
> I had
> My own song
> (Lorena Bruff)
> Write the tree's song.

323 Write a poem describing each stage your life has been through.

324 Read a poem, then write a poem in answer to the poet.

325 Write a poem, with a personal flavour, celebrating solitude.

326 Write a lullaby for a twenty-first century baby.

327 Write a poem in which you make an insincere apology for something you've done.

328 Write a poem about something whose beauty is visible only to you.

329 Write a poem in which you describe something, then give a number of examples of what it isn't.

330 Find a picture that interests you, then write a poem in which you converge with the people in the picture.

331 Write a poem inviting people to an exotic place full of fabulous sights and smells.

332 Write a poem about a scene where nothing is moving.

333 Write a poem about a wonderful experience in your life.

334 Write a poem entitled 'Choices' or 'Decisions'.

335 Write a parody of the song 'The Twelve Days of Christmas'.

336 Write a poem to the end of a season.

337 Write a poem beginning 'If the trees gushed blood'. (Mervyn Peake)

338 Describe the smells of Heaven.

339 Personify some great force, such as the ocean.

340 Write a poem thirty-four words long.

341 Write an ode to useless things.

342 Write a poem which ends with the death of an animal.

343 Take a bath by candlelight then write a poem about it.

344 The shortest poem ever written is claimed to be this, by Ogden Nash:
**'To my Goldfish'**
Wet
Pet.
Write one of approximately equal length.

345 W. H. Auden wrote a poem that began 'Tell me the truth about love.' Write a poem that begins 'Tell me the truth about . . .'

346 Write an answer to the poem above.

347 Describe a zoo in which there are cages for the abstract: e.g. for hatred, for the wind.

348 Write a poem that will be a cry for freedom.

349 Write a poem that begins 'The day our daughter/son was born . . .'

350 Write a poem showing someone's emotional state by the way they engage with a small object.

351 Write a poem about the worst thing that ever happened to you but don't say what it is.

352 'The landscape of my mind.' (Emma Davis)

353 These are all the common words that rhyme with '-ainly': plainly, mainly, sanely, vainly, urbanely, profanely, ungainly, humanely, insanely, inhumanely. Write a rhyming poem using some or all of these words.

354 These are all the common words that rhyme with '-aked': ached, baked, faked, caked, flaked, slaked, snaked, raked, braked, quaked. Write a rhyming poem using some or all of these words.

355 Write a poem about the smells boys like, or the smells girls like.

**356** Write in the form of a poem a recipe for a wild party.
**357** Write in the form of a poem a recipe for an afternoon designed to drive a teacher mad.

# Personal

**358** How did you find out the facts of life, and how did you react?

**359** Describe a time when you were in charge of something.

**360** Take a significant event in your life and write about it.

**361** Write about a time when you were frightened ... embarrassed ... angry ... proud ... jealous ... happy.

**362** Write a letter to the favourite stuffed toy you had when you were younger (or still have now.)

**363** Daydream for a while, then write.

**364** Go to a place that's very special to you and write there.

**365** How old or young in heart are you?

**366** Write about a memorable piece of writing you once did.

**367** Discuss the effect of fear on your life.

**368** Describe a time when an animal you've known has shown courage, loyalty, affection ...

**369** Write a page of complaints – have a good whinge about anything or everything.

**370** What's the best day's work you've ever done?

**371** Write about your grandparents.

**372** Describe the way you study or work.

**373** How do people make you feel guilty?

**374** Can you bear to be alone? Can you stand other people's company?

**375** Can you believe two contrary things at the same time?

**376** 'We had the experience but we missed the meaning.' (T. S. Eliot) Is this the story of your life so far?

377 'One must master the demons in oneself, not deny them.' What are your demons?

378 Explain why you're not a boring person. (Sue Germein) How do you bore yourself?

379 What makes you feel insecure? What is security for you?

380 Think of something you don't want to write about, then start writing about it.

381 Recall a time when you couldn't stop laughing.

382 Write a humorous description of your experiences on stage.

383 Write a piece which begins 'I am the one who . . .'

384 Write about a time when you should have spoken out but didn't.

385 Describe your relationship with your mirror.

386 'People talk, act, live as if they're never going to die. And what do they leave behind? Nothing, nothing but a mask.' (Bob Dylan) What mask will you leave behind?

387 'It's the greatest of all mistakes to do nothing because you can only do a little. Do what you can.' What can you do?

388 'Every punishment always brings its reward.' How has this been true in your life?

389 'The line is so thin between "I love you" and "I hate you".' Write about a time when you crossed that line.

390 Describe the most dangerous thing you've ever done.

391 'Almost all of our faults are more pardonable than the methods we use to try and hide them.' What are your faults and how do you try to hide them?

392 Think of your worst fear, then write a humorous piece about it.

393 'You can judge people's characters by the way they treat someone who can do nothing for them.' Evaluate your own character in the light of that remark.

**394** Describe an interruption that put spice into your life.

**395** What made you grow up?

**396** Justify your existence on this planet.

**397** Write about a time when you learned from a mistake.

**398** It's said that people average thirteen lies a week. What were your last thirteen?

**399** Write about a memorable fight you were in.

**400** 'You can't put anything in a closed fist.' When have you tried? What happened?

**401** Describe a time when you judged it wiser to conform.

**402** Write about a time when you covered up for someone.

**403** Describe a significant ceremony that you've experienced.

**404** What was your first temptation?

**405** Describe three incidents from your life – but make one of them a lie.

**406** Describe a day in your life.

**407** Write about a time when something said to you changed your life.

**408** Describe your relationship with your cousins.

**409** Is your imagination changing? Is it getting stronger or weaker – or don't those words apply?

**410** How has the mass media affected your life?

**411** Describe the most painful experience of your life.

**412** In what ways are you and your father alike? In what ways do you differ? How about you and your mother? Grandparents?

**413** Write the chapter headings for your autobiography. Make them stylish and intriguing.

**414** What's the worst thing about growing up?

**415** 'If we don't change our direction, we'll end up where we're headed.' Where are you headed? Do you want to change your direction?

**416** Write about a memorable photograph that you took or that you have.

417 In your life, have you been taught what to think or have you been taught how to think?

418 My sixteen-year relationship with God. (Change the number to match your age.)

419 Write about a time when you cried in public.

420 What are some things that have grossed you out?

421 Is there anything you don't believe?

422 Describe all the triumphs of your life.

423 'The biggest risk is to take none.' What recent risks have you taken?

424 'There are no trees on a sporting field, no rocks, nowhere to hide.' (Terry Wheeler, amended) Has this been your experience?

425 Describe how a broken promise had a strong effect on you.

426 'Education involves both a learning and an unlearning.' What have you needed to unlearn and learn? What do you still need to unlearn and learn?

427 Thanking my Mother for Piano Lessons. (poem title)

428 Write a detailed description of your body.

429 Do you have to love teachers to learn from them? (John Le Vert, paraphrased)

430 What have you contributed so far to your school or workplace? How has it benefited from your presence?

431 What's the most trouble you've ever been in?

432 How do you react (if at all) to any of these words: Collingwood Magpies/Cricket/Brisbane Broncos?

433 'It's important to be involved in something bigger than oneself.' Are you?

434 Describe the first incident you can clearly remember.

435 What's the most memorable lesson you've had?

436 'I hate being thirteen,' she said. 'See? I'm weird,' he murmured. 'I love it.' (Tim Winton, *Lockie Leonard, Human Torpedo*) What do you think of the age you are now? What's been your favourite age?

437 State the code you live by. List your principles.

**438** Tell of a time when you were treated unfairly. Then retell the same episode from the other person's/people's point of view.

**439** What would be the best and worst ways to die?

**440** 'Hell is the denial of the ordinary.' (John Ciardi) Do you agree? Design your personal hell.

**441** Write a guide to self-improvement.

**442** Write about an illness or injury you've had.

**443** What things do you do because they're good for you, even though you don't enjoy them?

**444** What are your bad habits?

**445** What are your responsibilities?

**446** How do you feel underwater?

**447** How do you feel in a crowd?

**448** Describe an experience that caused you to form or acquire a particular belief.

**449** Describe a motel experience you've had – humorously perhaps.

**450** Write your memories of the birth of one of your siblings.

**451** 'You have not converted people just because you have silenced them.' Tell of a time when you were silenced but not converted.

**452** List all the things you believe in.

**453** State a belief you hold strongly and explain why you believe it.

**454** How well do your parents know you?

**455** Do you believe in ghosts? Telepathy? Poltergeists? ESP? Seances?

**456** Who are your heroes and why? If you don't have any, why is that?

**457** What's the most memorable dream you've ever had?

**458** When was the last time you lost your temper?

**459** Describe a time when someone helped you.

**460** Describe a time when you've helped someone.

**461** Have you had a happy childhood?

462 Recount any experiences you've had with the police, and describe your feelings about the police generally.

463 Describe a time when telling the truth would have been a better idea than lying.

464 Describe a camping or hiking experience you've had.

465 What particular skill do you most lack? How do you feel about it?

466 What on-going sore points are there between you and your parent/s?

467 As a child, what things were you told (by adults) that you later found were untrue? How do you feel about those deceptions now?

468 What are some times when you've gone to extremes to win?

469 'Gone but not forgotten.'

470 What adult achievements of yours would most please your parents? What would most disappoint them?

471 Describe a time when you conquered a fear.

472 Describe a time when you got into trouble, but you were innocent.

473 What are your feelings about nakedness?

474 What do you think the perfect family would be like?

475 Tell of a time when you did your best but still didn't succeed.

476 What's the biggest disaster you ever caused?

477 What do you think would be the best and worst things about going to boarding school?

478 'If only . . .' Continue from this start.

479 Describe the worst fight you ever had with a friend.

480 What's it like to have a parent cry?

481 Describe something you used to believe in but now don't.

482 Recall a time when a lot of people laughed at you.

483 Recall the last time you couldn't get to sleep at night.

484 'Obstacles are a stimulus to him/her.' Is that true for you? Give examples.

**485** 'Growing up beats throwing up.' Do you agree?

**486** Describe a character who's the complete opposite to you.

**487** The first time I . . .

**488** The last day.

**489** 'Beaten by the referee.' (or umpire)

**490** 'The Black Sheep of Our Family.'

**491** Describe an obsession you've had (or still have).

**492** You've just taken a truth pill. Now write about the last fight you were in, or the last time you got in trouble, or the last time you fell in love.

**493** Write a piece which shows your real self, your public self, and your imagined self.

**494** Where is your home? Give an abstract or creative response to this question.

**495** Write what it means to be a man/woman.

**496** 'Fat is a four letter word.'

**497** Describe yourself through the eyes of someone who's deaf and blind.

**498** Who's the biggest friend you ever had?

**499** Observe an animal for an hour, then write a comparison between it and human beings.

**500** Do something you've never done before and write about it.

**501** Choose something that's happened recently that you think will be of historical importance. Describe what happened and how you'll explain it to your children.

# Limits

502 Write a one hundred-word story in which no word is repeated.

503 Write your life story in fourteen words exactly. Make it stylish!

504 Write a one hundred-word story in which no word is more than four letters long.

505 Write a complete story of exactly fifty words, no more, no less. It should have a beginning, a middle and an end.

506 Write a story in which every word is a monosyllable.

507 Describe an argument in which no words are exchanged.

508 Write about a battle in which no shots are fired ... or only one shot is fired.

509 Write about a war in which no-one dies.

510 Define common objects, ideas or feelings in less than twenty words. Be specific. Examples: justice, television, books, matchboxes, war.

511 Take a tiny piece of paper, about the size of a postage stamp, and write the longest story you can on it, front and back.

512 Write a one hundred-word story in which the letter 'e' is not used.

513 Write as many three-word phrases as you can in which each word begins with the letter R ... or S ... or H ...

514 Write a story in which you incorporate as many movie titles as possible. Aim for at least twenty. ('The *Pretty Woman* got covered in *Grease* by *Dr Strangelove* when he treated her *Saturday Night Fever* ... ')

515 Describe an object or place (such as a telephone or a zoo) in words of one syllable.

**516** Write a story that consists entirely of dialogue.

**517** Write a conversation where each sentence has to start with the next letter of the alphabet. (Adapted from 'Whose Line is it Anyway?')

**518** Write a conversation where each speaks sentences of a fixed number of words – 1, 2, 3, 4, or 5. (Adapted from 'Whose Line is it Anyway?')

**519** Write about a death in words of one syllable.

**520** Write a story in which every word contains the letter 'a'.

**521** Spend five minutes writing about the ocean, then repeat without using any of the words you used in the first piece.

# Developing Skills

**522** Write a spaceship-from-another planet story with all the cliches, then write one without them.

**523** Describe yourself from the point of view of an enemy, a friend, a parent, a teacher, a sibling, your bus-driver.

**524** Show how someone's feeling by the way they react to the place they're in.

**525** Write down thirty different details about a common object – T-shirt or a pen or a pet.

**526** Eat an orange, recording details of the taste of each part; including the peel and pips. Record the smells and feel of each part too.

**527** Suck on a sweet slowly, recording the way the taste changes.

**528** Observe an ant for five minutes, writing a description of it. Move fifty metres, find another ant and repeat the exercise.

**529** Write a piece in a style quite different to the way you normally write.

**530** Cut out a frame of paper or cardboard, place it in an interesting spot, then write about everything you see in that frame.

**531** Write a story in which two events happen simultaneously.

**532** Describe yourself (or someone else) without mentioning your physical appearance.

**533** Invent a character then describe her or his bathroom.

**534** Write a passage of dialogue in which it is obvious which speakers are male and which are female.

**535** If one is stone cold, emotionally, and ten is over the top, try describing the same sequence of events several different times, taking a different number as your guide each time.

**536** Write a story which consists of several scenes. Go into each scene as late as you can and get out of each one as soon as possible.

**537** Write a scene then rewrite it three times with three different emotions.

**538** What is the hardest emotion to write about? Write a story which explores it.

**539** Describe something from extremely close-up.

**540** Describe a really funny episode in your life. Then rewrite it showing the sadness in it.

**541** Write a set of instructions for removing a tiger from your kitchen. (David Inman)

**542** In a piece of descriptive writing show us where we are by reference to three objects. Be subtle.

**543** Write a piece in which you gradually create a sense of menace.

**544** Write a conversation during which people keep touching each other in different ways.

**545** Write a conversation during which the speakers are constantly touching or using objects.

**546** Where one is cool to the point of coldness and ten is wildly hysterical, write a sentence for each number between one and ten.

**547** Write a conversation which consists entirely of questions.

**548** Write a critical review of a play or a film you've seen recently.

**549** Write a set of instructions, explaining to kids how to get their own way with their parents.

**550** Describe an ordinary, everyday scene that has, however, one disturbing element.

**551** Describe a scene in which there is a strong contrast or something that you wouldn't normally expect to find. (Make sure there's a purpose to the contrast.)

**552** Describe something from an unusual perspective, without telling us what it is.

**553** Write about a scene that most people wouldn't consider worthy of attention (and so it is virtually invisible to them).

**554** Describe an argument or conflict between a male and female, taking the female point of view if you're male or the male point of view if you're female.

**555** 'Freeze' a dramatic scene and describe it in words. Don't worry about the prelude and sequel: just describe the scene itself.

**556** Describe a scene in which there is only a moment of action: a very small activity.

**557** Describe a scene in which there is balance – movement balancing something that is still, perhaps.

**558** Write a passage in which something happens that seems real ... yet when we think about it, it must be impossible.

**559** Describe a scene which is dominated by rich, intense colour.

**560** Describe a scene in which something enigmatic yet intense is happening. Don't tell us what is happening.

**561** Write about the varied reactions of different people to an event without telling us what the event is.

**562** Describe a scene in which there is close scrutiny of every detail.

**563** Spend an hour taking a journey of fifty metres, writing about it as you go.

**564** Observe something organic for a week, writing about it each day. (Peg Cherry)

**565** Isolate a small patch of ground, shrink yourself to the size of a baby ant and take a journey through this transformed world.

**566** Describe someone walking their dog, and in doing so give us a good understanding of their personality.

**567** Describe someone drinking coffee, and in doing so give us a good understanding of their personality.

**568** Describe someone in a shop, and in doing so give us a good understanding of their personality.

**569** Start writing a scene. Every few minutes have someone call out an emotion; immediately incorporate that emotion into the scene. (Adapted from 'Whose Line is it Anyway?')

**570** Write in the voice of someone naive.

**571** Write in the voice of someone negative.

**572** Write ten irresistible opening sentences.

**573** Write a piece where we become aware that the person's crying – but you never tell us that.

**574** Write a piece in which two things are happening at once.

**575** Write a scene with you and a character as totally unlike you as you can get, and put the two of you in a situation: e.g. a teacher puts you and the other person together, over your objections, to work on an assignment.

**576** Write a speech for a person of high status who is suddenly interrupted in the middle of it. (Alan Aykbourn)

**577** Write a speech where someone of low status suddenly finds he/she's allowed to speak uninterrupted.

**578** Describe someone driving along or making coffee, but something else is happening in their life.

**579** Write the story of Adam and Eve from the points-of-view of Adam, Eve, the snake and God.

**580** Write a description of someone whose whole life is controlled by TV ads.

**581** Write a monologue where someone starts off lying but gradually becomes honest.

**582** Explain God in the style of two construction workers having a conversation, or two little kids.

**583** Write a story for little kids that will explain death to them.

**584** Write an argument where every insult is accompanied

by a term of endearment (the more original the
better).

**585** Write a scene in which someone undergoes a great
transformation.

# Letters

**586** Write a letter to someone, thanking them for a bizarre gift.

**587** Write a letter to an angel ... your personal angel perhaps.

**588** Write a letter to a cloud, as you lie on the grass, on your back.

**589** Try a letter to a flower, a tree or the moon.

**590** Write a series of letters between you and your conscience.

**591** Write a series of letters between you and Santa.

**592** Write a series of letters between you and someone who's died.

**593** Write a letter to yourself, to be read in five years.

**594** Write a letter to yourself, to be read in fifty years.

**595** Write a letter to God.

**596** Write a letter to your parent/s, thanking them for something.

**597** Write a letter to another member of the class.

**598** Write a letter to one of your parents. Give it to them or not, as you choose. But say the things you really want to say.

**599** Write a letter to the Prime Minister, expressing what it is like to be a young person in Australia today.

**600** Write a letter to a real person, explaining what you find difficult about writing.

# Conclusion

Every writer approaches writing differently. People who hand you a list of rules and tell you that they've just given you the secrets of writing aren't doing you a favour. You have to work out your own way. Ernest Hemingway wrote all his novels on his feet, literally. He believed he functioned best while standing. That worked for him, fine. Try it if you want. If it doesn't work for you, try something else. When Alexander Dumas got writer's block he called the servants, undressed, and had himself locked naked into a small room with just a pen and paper. He figured the only thing he could do in the room was to write. Well, that's what he said he was doing. Maybe he didn't have as much imagination as we thought.

Lots of people stress a sense of audience as important for writers. I have quite a sense of audience when I write, but many writers don't. Ursula LeGuin, for one, is on record as saying that she doesn't think about it at all. Robert Cormier often tells the story of how he wrote *The Chocolate War* and sent it to his agent, who read it, rang him and said: 'So you've written a novel for young adults?'

'Oh,' said Cormier, 'have I?'

Alan Garner is a writer I admire. On the blurb of one of his books he describes how the most important element in writing for him is to have the book's last paragraph clear before he starts. He gets that last paragraph word perfect. That's the complete opposite to me. I can't start until the first paragraph or the first page is clear. I need to get the right tone for it; after that I'm fine. As I've said elsewhere in this book, I need to have the voice of the main characters. I usually have no idea how the book will end.

There are no rules in writing. There are conventions, some of them strong, but there are no rules. There's a convention, for example, that every sentence should finish with a full-stop. But once you understand these conventions and all their subtleties, you should consider yourself free to break them. You might run sentences together without full-stops, without much punctuation at all, to convey a sense of rapid thinking, fear or breathlessness:

**If I move round here a bit she might turn and notice me gotta look cool what's she looking at, the surf? might just make a comment here something about the waves what can I say that'll be so dazzling she'll look at me differently prove I'm not boring, not a nerd oh God wish I wasn't sweating so much OK here goes: 'Um, do you think it's going to rain?'**

I want to state and restate some simple principles of writing that I consider to be important. But they still shouldn't be considered rules.

Be honest.

Take risks.

Find your own voice.

Write and write and write and write.

Explore inner lives.

Be specific.

Feel the energy that burns in every word.

Understate.

Be disciplined.

Writing continues to be a noble, wonderful, demanding, exasperating pastime. A teacher in Melbourne told me the other day of a poem that one of her students had read. The student came to her, waving the poem excitedly. 'At last!' she said. 'I've found a poem that understands me!'

May it be given to you to write such a poem.

# Learn great new writing skills, with John Marsden

**You are invited to spend a few days with John Marsden at one of Australia's most beautiful properties.**

The Tye Estate is just 25 minutes from Melbourne's Tullamarine Airport, and is perfectly set up for writing camps and other activities.

Every school holidays, John takes writing and drama camps, where you can improve your skills, make new friends, expand your thinking, and have a huge heap of fun.

Accommodation is modern and comfortable; meals are far removed from the shepherd's pie they gave you at your last school camp, and supervision is by friendly and experienced staff.

Between the workshops with John, you can explore 850 acres of spectacular bush, looking out for rare and highly endangered species like Tiger Quolls and Powerful Owls, as well as koalas, platypuses, wedgetail eagles, kangaroos and wallabies.

Mountain bikes, bushwalking, orienteering, and a picnic at nearby Hanging Rock, are among the highlights of your memorable stay at the Tye Estate.

School groups in term time are also welcome.

For details, write to:

The Tye Estate
RMB 1250
ROMSEY
VICTORIA 3434

Or fax: (61) 03 54 270395
Phone: (61) 03 54 270384